Counseling Employees

Counseling Employees

by

EARL M. BOWLER

Coördinator, Public Service Occupations
Bureau of Industrial and Business Training
Extension Division   The University of Texas

and

FRANCES TRIGG DAWSON

Personnel Consultant and Director of
Vocational Education
Elon College   North Carolina

New York

PRENTICE-HALL, INC.

1948

Foreword

A SYSTEMATIC employee counseling program was seldom found —and perhaps not needed—in the industrial plant of a few decades ago. Employees were in close personal touch not only with their immediate supervisors but frequently with higher levels of management, even to the owner or owners of the company. This close contact provided for an informal interchange of ideas, feelings, and points of view without a systematic employee counseling program. Counseling occurred, to be sure, and often very excellent counseling, but there were no persons hired specifically as counselors with the counseling function designated as their job.

Modern industrial organization has developed to a point where the relationship between employee and supervisor has often become more and more remote, in spite of the serious and concentrated efforts of many managements to preserve the former close relationship through a systematic program of supervisory training. A good many managements—managements known for their attention to promising developments in the field of industrial relations—are attempting to regain a closer employee-employer relationship through a systematic employee counseling program. Such a program is not without dangers and will not escape the criticism of those who feel that it is a reversion to a type of paternalism that is frowned upon not only by organized labor but by many managements as well. Yet many companies that have carefully prepared and put into operation a counseling program have found the effort to be very much worthwhile—and employees likewise have profited from and are enthusiastic about this addition to the industrial relations services of their plants.

The present book is a much needed systematic coverage of current practice in the field of personnel counseling. Descriptions of many operating counseling programs are included and these are evaluated in terms of general principles which have come from the extensive experience of the authors. The book will be of real value to companies operating or contemplating the installation of a counseling program; to industrial relations directors who are interested in a concise and accurate summary of what other companies have done in this field; and to students of personnel, industrial relations, and industrial psychology.

JOSEPH TIFFIN

Preface

THIS BOOK deals with the functioning of counselors in employee adjustment, in personnel, and in industrial relations. Many employee counselors have expressed the desire for a handbook written by practical people, in down-to-earth style. This book is an answer to that well-founded wish; it has been prepared to help all counselors do a better job.

Counseling as an industrial relations tool is so new that the principles and practices have not yet reached the smooth-running perfection that characterizes many other functions of an organization. A great deal that has been written is scattered through leaflets, pamphlets and bulletins. To find specific advice and suggestions in these publications is at best an arduous task.

Counseling is not a fad; it is a practice born of necessity. Morale and satisfaction are so closely related to adjustment that it is amazing that we have so long successfully operated large organizations without a liaison between the man on the machine or the girl in the stock room, and the man with the policy pen. Our fast growth as an industrial nation has given us little time to be analytical with our personnel problems, but the urgencies of stepped-up production have compelled us to seek the solution to some of the more acute troubles. As a result, the counselor has emerged as a "must" in the field of industrial and human relations.

Today it is universally recognized that there must be a specialist within the personnel department who is capable of helping workers help themselves. This book discusses the ways and means of dealing with these many-sided problems.

Specialization is the order of the day, and the employee with acute personal difficulties is keenly aware of the quality of assistance given him in solving his problems. Experience has shown that workers return time and again to reliable sources for sound advice. This growing desire for expert assistance has added impetus to counseling as a specialized service and as an adjustment tool. Counseling will continue to increase in favor so long as it renders valuable service to the individual worker.

Experimentation and exploration in industrial relations is still going on. In the past the foreman or the supervisor was expected to diagnose the personnel difficulties and prescribe the cure that would bring production back to normal. Life was more simple, and an experienced foreman could do quite well by drawing upon his own experience to bridge the difficulty. However, the problems of the individual worker have become increasingly complex both within and without the plant. This only serves to emphasize any ineptness on the part of foremen or supervisors in handling the workers' problems, because the former are faced with increasingly complex conditions while the workers are experiencing newer benefits and more advantages.

Localized attempts have been made to maintain an open-door management policy. Where this arrangement has been tried by management, unrelated decisions are frequently made which result in unsound personnel policies and favoritism. Workers are quick to spot the failings and weaknesses of the one-man organization.

Employers are sensing the advantages of counseling as the answer to many of their knotty problems. The expanding realization of its value in building up morale, avoiding costly labor difficulties, and increasing the efficiency and therefore the production of the workers, has firmly established counseling within the field of personnel administration.

Acknowledgments

During the time *Counseling Employees* was in preparation, many individuals gave generously of their time and energy to the end that many worthwhile ideas might be crystallized in print. The authors are very grateful to Dr. Robert L. Sutherland, Director of the Hogg Foundation for Mental Hygiene, The University of Texas, for his interest in the undertaking and for his suggestions of manuscript reviewers.   To W. H. Brentlinger, Professor of Psychology, The University of Texas, we offer our sincere thanks for reviewing early drafts of the manuscript and for making helpful suggestions that permitted us to make the book more adaptable as a text in the field of personnel work.   Our appreciation is expressed to Dr. Natalie Kneeland, Professor, Distributive Education, William and Mary College, for her encouragement and stimulation.   Whatever merit this work possesses we attribute to the invaluable suggestions given by these, our friends.

THE AUTHORS

Contents

WHY COUNSEL EMPLOYEES?

SPECIAL PHASES OF COUNSELING

THE COUNSELOR'S JOB

THE COUNSELING PROGRAM

Why Counsel Employees?

THERE have been many attempts to define and delimit counseling. In operating personnel programs, there will always be a question as to where the personnel management function ends and where the counseling function begins. Possibly, all personnel department activities are of a counseling nature. However, this description would not establish satisfactory criteria for judging the nature of counseling. Many who contact the personnel department are handled in routine fashion with no special service rendered that could be considered to be of an *adjustment* nature.

Counseling and adjustment are so closely related that any definition of the service rendered must use or imply the word, *adjustment*. One definition which seems to describe adequately the work of the industrial counselor follows: *Counseling is the rendering of a specialized service in connection with occupational planning, placement, or adjustment which is aimed at prevention, solution, or betterment of a problem for an individual or a group.* Counseling is a staff function which strengthens the position of middle management with the workers in the organization. The counselor who renders greatest service needs no authority of his own. He functions through individuals in authority while helping workers to help themselves.

Job and Occupational Adjustment

The occupational adjustment phases of the definition imply that the worker is employed on a job he is qualified to do, that the work is to his liking, meets his needs, and that the worker is satisfactory to his employer. The definition given does not limit counseling to plant problems. Any condition, situation, or problem that may be reflected in the quality or quantity of an employee's output is considered to be within the scope of the counseling program.

The titles and the scope of duties of persons employed to render counseling services in private industry vary greatly. A few of the more common designations are: Counselor, Supervisor, Coordinator, Employment Manager, Forelady, Group Leader, Head Operator, Nurse, Interviewer, Instructor, Matron, Personnel Assistant, and Personnel Representative. Duties range all the way from those of employment manager with the authority to hire, discipline, and fire, to those of the counselor who is an adviser without authority to take any action.

Problems flow to the counselor from many sources. A worker who is failing to make the necessary job adjustment may come to the counselor for help. A foreman who has spotted decreasing output and flagging interest on the part of an individual may report the situation to the counselor. A fellow worker may notify the counselor of the fact that things are not well with his coworker. The counselor as he moves about the plant also observes conditions needing adjustment.[1]

The magnitude of the problems brought to the counselor for adjustment varies greatly. Some situations are only a little off balance. Timekeeping errors, payroll deductions, and policy interpretations are typical problems where merely putting the worker in contact with the right person completes the adjustment. In such cases, the counselor must follow-up to make certain that the worker has received satisfaction as a result of the contacts made. However, not all problems arising in the plant are this simple.

Many of the more serious problems are deep-seated, and traceable to minor irritations glossed over until someone takes a defi-

---

[1] The problems described in the text do not exist in industrial plants alone. For a discussion of problems in governmental agencies see: H. E. Eisler, "Personnel Counseling Obviously Needed," *Personnel Journal*, December, 1943, pages 140-146. New York: Personnel Research Federation.

nite stand. Handling situations of this kind demands the use of a problem solving technique described later. Obviously, the action taken by the counselor should result in better employee understanding and improved worker adjustment. For example, consider the situation of Mike Malloy. Mike was a satisfactory worker whose assignments were completed on schedule; the quality of his work was above average; there was seldom any conversation or "horseplay" around his work station. Everyone spoke to Mike as they came to work and he seemed to have the respect of the group. Fellow workers neither especially liked nor disliked him. No one knew his outside interests or problems because he was not a person who told his troubles or personal affairs to his associates. One day the supervisor noticed that Mike was doing a job the long and hard way and was thereby wasting materials. The supervisor was an active member of various training programs and knew certain short cuts that apparently Mike had not discovered. He walked over and said: "Mike, let me show you a trick that will make that job much easier and also save on the material used."

Mike replied: "I'm doing all right. I don't waste material."

The supervisor thought he detected a curtness in Mike's voice, but he continued, "I know a short cut that will save you a lot of time and energy as well as material. Let me show you."

Mike came back with: "Listen, I don't need any help. When I do, I'll ask for it. You don't have to pick on me."

The supervisor answered: "Mike, I am trying to help you. You don't need to get sore. We've got to keep a good record in this department."

Mike was getting red-faced by now and said: "I tend to my own business around here, don't I? I don't hand you no stuff, do I? Well, I ain't taking no gaff either, see?"

The conversation continued in a heated way for a short time, then the foreman intervened. He simply remarked: "Break it up, boys," and the supervisor and foreman walked away. Enough had been said on both sides so that the matter could not be dropped. The foreman asked the counselor to talk to both the supervisor and Mike and get to the bottom of the trouble.

The supervisor could give no reason for the sudden outburst from Mike. He stated the facts about Mike's work record and remarked that Mike was the lone wolf type who tended to his own business. The counselor then scheduled a meeting with Mike. All this was done within two hours after the upsetting incident occurred.

In these situations timing is important. There was a two-hour cooling off period for Mike, and the counselor had a chance to look over the records of both men prior to talking with them. Mike's record has already been mentioned. The supervisor's record was average. He was satisfactory but not outstanding in meeting production schedules and dealing with those persons under his supervision. He apparently had no serious problems of his own.

Mike was sent by the foreman to the counselor and was aware that the supervisor had already talked with the counselor. The counselor asked Mike to be seated. (*Note*: There had been no contact between Mike and the counselor since the indoctrination program when Mike was first employed.) Several important facts were brought out during the conversation between Mike and the counselor.

1. During the first week of employment, Mike had overheard a fellow employee ask the supervisor, "What's the new guy's name?" The supervisor answered, "Mike Malloy." The employee remarked, "Another damned church-goer, I suppose."

The supervisor had not answered the employee and Mike had interpreted this as uncomplimentary. He felt that the supervisor and fellow employees did not like persons of the Catholic faith. His conclusion disturbed him because he was faithful in church attendance and in meeting his obligations to his religion. He also valued his job and had kept still. He had been especially cautious in his remarks to others and had acquired the reputation of being quiet.

2. About a month after Mike started to work, one of the fellows who had been employed for several years was quitting. The department members planned a little farewell party for him. Mike was invited but did not accept. His wife was ill at the time, but when he had given this explanation of his refusal the fellows had not believed him. They labeled Mike as being unsociable and forgot the incident.

3. The supervisor had found it easy to talk with most of the fellows and while he always spoke in a friendly way to Mike, he did not bother to make conversation with him. When the supervisor had joked with any of the men, Mike felt a personal discrimination.

4. At former jobs, Mike had been a leader.

5. He wanted attention from his fellow workers.

6. Fear of ridicule and losing his job because of his religion had caused him to be quiet when he first started to work, and the misunderstandings which had developed because of these first remarks had created a situation which needed only one flick of irritation to cause an explosion.

7. Mike had not felt that he "belonged" to the group. He felt like an outsider.

8. When a newer (more recently hired) employee was asked to be Chairman of the Red Cross Drive, Mike had taken it as a personal insult.

9. He imagined that many of the other fellows were getting the breaks on job assignments and his general dissatisfaction was built up until on the day when the supervisor was attempting to be of assistance, Mike had revolted.

10. The knowledge of a short cut in job performance and of saving material was something that Mike admitted he would have appreciated if there had not been a deep-seated problem which caused him to resent being approached.

The problems of Mike Malloy were resolved in the following manner: first, Mike was made aware, very definitely, that the company had no ill feelings towards any religion. It was pointed out that the vice-president of the company was of the same faith as Mike.   Arrangements were soon made by the counselor for these two men to meet and Mike was made to feel much more at ease about his religious background.   An understanding was reached between the supervisor and Mike.   The slights felt so keenly by Mike were clarified to his satisfaction.   Shortly after the interview, Mike was appointed to a job on the workers' Cafeteria Committee.   Fellow workers gradually became aware that Mike was not an unsociable person.   From this point on, Mike proved to be one of the best workmen in the department.

If you are not actively engaged in personnel work you might rightfully ask the question, "How does counseling and worker adjustment affect me?"   As a consumer, you should know that the price tags on the products you buy reflect, in a measure, the quality of the counseling in the industry manufacturing that product.   Inadequate quantities and poor quality are frequently the work of poorly adjusted employees.   In this age of mechanization the consuming public has a larger stake in the smooth operations of an industrial plant than we realize.

The worker and employer lose heavily, too, when counseling is not a part of the industrial relations program.   If the worker has a problem, real or imaginary, he gets satisfaction one way or another.   Either someone in the plant adjusts the matter to the worker's satisfaction or he quits.   Time lost between jobs comes out of the worker's pocket.   Material wasted and production lost during the breaking-in period on a new job come out of the employer's pocket.   The cost of labor turnover was frequently demonstrated in meeting and solving war production problems.

Turnover cost is high in itself, but the *slowdown* of workers can be more costly.   A poorly adjusted worker who hangs on not knowing what to do about his situation can create a greater financial burden than the individual who quits and must be replaced. Counseling can prevent many such problems from arising.   It is also a solution for worker dissatisfaction resulting from a multiplicity of other situations that demand satisfactory answers.

Worker satisfaction is linked closely with occupational adjustment, and where excessive turnover, slowdowns, or other signals indicate an impending breakdown, the counselor gets to the source of the trouble.   For example, he may check the adequacy of the selection and placement factors, the effectiveness of the induction program, the quality of on-the-job orientation, the timeliness of safety training, and the manner of supervision.   Counselors, by promoting better occupational adjustment of workers, can assist management in wisely using one of its most valuable assets—the employee.

As industry grows and expands, the number and kinds of jobs increase.   Opportunities for adequate guidance and counsel are limited to a small portion of the population living in the larger cities where school programs attempt to satisfy the need.   Economic factors frequently require a worker to take any available job regardless of his own preferences.   The lack of accurate information about an occupation or a specific job, facts which a counselor could give, might mean the difference between hiring a person who is adapted for the job and employing an individual who becomes dismayed because he has failed to find the right niche.

Frequent industrial changes have their effect upon workers, too.   New processes and materials demanding new skills and work techniques also contribute to the workers' problems.   Individuals who have recently become adjusted to their jobs often find the technical scene shifted so that they are once more left behind.   If stability is important to the worker, it is likewise important to the employer.   Situations affecting the worker also affect production.   Counselors are the key to occupational adjustment, and they have a place in maintaining the production force at a constant level of performance.

The following diagram shows where the counselor fits into the job adjustment situation when a problem blocks the line of adjustment between the worker and the job.   When the occupational line fails to permit free flow of satisfaction between worker and job, contact is made possible by a counselor who bridges the gap.   The counselor supplies the needed contact which brings the worker into adjustment with either his present job or a new one.

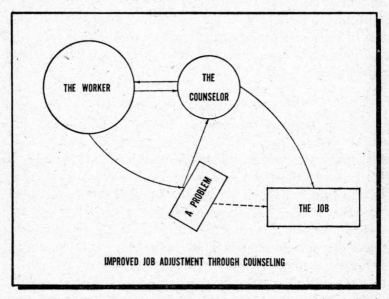

IMPROVED JOB ADJUSTMENT THROUGH COUNSELING

THE SERVICES OF A COUNSELOR AID IN RAPID AND COMPLETE JOB ADJUSTMENT OF WORKERS.

The occupational adjustment line is important, and it is strongest when (1) the job is satisfactory to the worker; (2) the worker is happy in what he is doing; (3) the worker is qualified for the job; (4) adequate supervision is maintained.

In the simplest adjustment situation, three steps are involved.

1. The counselor SPOTS the problem.
2. He makes a DEFINITE APPOINTMENT for the worker or supervisor with the person who can supply information that will clear up the situation.
3. The counselor FOLLOWS-UP to see that his action results in the satisfactory adjustment of the worker to the job.

Complex problems require the more comprehensive treatment discussed on page 189. It has been pointed out that the worker, the employer, and the public stand to lose when the worker fails in his adjustment to the job. This failure may be the result of something the worker does or does not do, or it may be the result of factors completely beyond the control of the worker. Regardless of the source of the blocking in the job adjustment line, the counselor is the key person in the restoration of the worker's job satisfaction.

The Importance of Job Satisfaction

Job satisfaction is the feeling of well-being that comes to a worker when he knows his specific assignment was tailor-made for him. There are those who believe that wages alone form the basis for all job pleasure and motivation. Wages, it is true, play an important role in worker adjustment, but they are not the sole reason for complete job satisfaction.

The feeling of security that comes from steady employment under favorable working conditions has been mentioned in many industrial relations surveys as an important factor. Considerate treatment by supervisors and foremen rates above all else in the minds of many workers as the important factor for happiness on the job. The feeling of "belonging" is one of our strongest motivating forces. Progressive management, recognizing the potency of this driving force, has capitalized upon it through training programs which insure that its foremen treat workers as individuals.

In the matter of job gratification, the alert counselor, with his fingers on the pulse of the workers, can aid management to correct practices which are the source of irritations leading to possible trouble.[2]

Counselors, when they are members of the personnel depart-

---

[2] As much as 60 per cent of all job dissatisfaction has been attributed to the inability of the individual to adjust himself emotionally. James F. Bender, "Emotional Adjustment of Workers," *Personnel Journal,* February, 1944, pages 301-307.

ment, may spend a major portion of each working day with individuals who have relatively simple adjustments to make.   For example, they may (1) Talk with employees who do not understand, or fail to interpret correctly, a plant-wide rule or posted regulation.   (2) Clarify such common misunderstandings as those that arise from promotional policies based upon departmental or plant-wide seniority.   (3) Give information about services and facilities available to employees: schools, legal advisers, financial institutions, and the like.   (4) Help supervisors and foremen to answer specific questions of company policy on a variety of matters including tardiness, loafing on the job, absenteeism, and other infractions indulged in by a small group of habitual offenders.[3]

Simple changes which help the workers to feel that management is interested in their welfare often bring about improved industrial relations.   The speed with which obviously needed changes are made serves as a good barometer of the progressiveness of the industrial relations program in a plant.   Employment practices that strive to match the qualifications of the worker to the demands of the job keep worker dissatisfaction to a minimum.[4] Where individuals have proved to be maladjusted in their job assignments, the counselor, after consultation with the supervisor, may suggest the use of transfer procedure.   The counselor can assist the hiring officer in establishing an adequate system of guidance, testing, selection, and placement within the plant. Lacking the possibilities of such a program within the organization, help on matters of this nature may be obtained from State Employment Services, the Department of Labor, colleges, and private industrial psychologists.

---

[3] There are those who would divide counseling into handling miscellaneous duties and handling psychological problems with specialists in each field.   This setup is described by Nathaniel Cantor and John C. Bonning in "Functions of Personnel Counselors," *Personnel Journal,* September, 1944, pages 104-110.

[4] Well-adjusted workers are efficient workers.   The margin of difference between a successful enterprise and an unsuccessful one frequently hinges upon the efficiency of the workers.   Discussion is carried further by: C. F. McPeak, in "Help Workers to the Right Job," *Personnel Journal,* February, 1943, pages 289-294.

Testing programs frequently prove that workers possess capacities far beyond that demanded by the job they are holding. If up-graded to more challenging jobs, such workers may remain in the employ of the company, and not infrequently be eventually promoted to supervisory positions. Conversely, employees not capable of performing their present duties may be transferred to jobs where the requirements, pressure, and the tension are less. Attention to details of this kind tends to keep in balance many factors, which, when left to chance, eventually result in the need for corrective measures.

A lack of interest, day-dreaming, dawdling, and woolgathering are additional evidences of inadequate job satisfaction. Under such conditions, production may be far from optimum, and the worker may be far from happy. The accident rate tends to climb when the job does not challenge the worker.

Great steam turbines are controlled by a governor which keeps the machine operating at a constant speed, and huge gyroscopes keep ocean liners on an even keel. The counselor may be compared to the devices that keep such costly machines in balance. How smoothly the personnel machine functions depends largely upon how well it is cared for and how frequently it is adjusted to existing conditions. Interest and job satisfaction are closely associated. Every worker should feel that his work challenges him to do his best. He needs the feeling that success is attainable.

The counselor has an important function in balancing the human relationships existing in an organization. He should not be visualized as an all-wise and all-knowing person, however. Open-mindedness in receiving information and discreetness in passing along factual material are strong factors for his success in counseling.

The Individual and His Rights

Few will deny that a worker has certain rights that management should not ignore. Some of the rights demanded by workers actually lie beyond the jurisdiction of the plant program and careful reasoning will reveal the fallacy of taking issue with the worker over them. In general, workers who plead for their rights have reference to some incident involving racial, political, religious, personal or union activity.[5] Seasoned counselors know that when management plans to enter these spheres of worker activity, it should be done only after careful planning and research indicate that the action is justified.

Job satisfaction tends to improve worker morale; transgression of worker rights tends to deplete morale. Cases involving rights are usually so deep-seated that they are not easily spotted; if not quickly discovered and rectified, a full-blown problem may develop. The counselor with a warm friendly attitude should be able to gain the worker's confidence and get at the heart of the real or imagined grievance.

Frequently, the opportunity to "blow off steam" is the safety valve that answers the employee's hunger to be heard on the subject bothering him. After asserting his rights, his tension is released and little more is heard. The kindly ear or listening post technique of a skillful counselor can instill in the employee the feeling that management is vitally interested in his well-being.

Problems involving the in-plant rights of an employee require square dealing. Supervisors trained to handle industrial relations problems are a preventive that will keep many minor situations under control. Thus controlled, these situations are kept from reaching the assertion stage. If conditions within the plant are so bad that undesirable situations are permitted to continue until individuals demand their rights, management should take prompt, vigorous action to establish or restore satisfactory industrial relations.

---

[5] Temperament and emotion may blind a worker to the real issues. The inability of a worker to make the necessary job adjustments may be the exciting cause behind the desire to assert one's "rights" too frequently. The matter of temperament among workers is further discussed by D. G. Humm and G. W. Wadsworth, Jr., in "Temperament in Industry," *Personnel Journal,* March, 1943, pages 314-319.

Can We Classify Counselees?

Counselees may be grouped in a variety of classifications depending upon the type analysis to be made. For example, counseling is available to both employed and unemployed individuals. Problems confronting the counselees may be the basis for classification; two general problem categories are the in-plant and out-plant types. An in-plant problem might be that of a worker feeling that the foreman does not like him, while an out-plant problem might be that of a worker failing to show up for work because of drunkenness.

Those problems which involve a mild adjustment of the individual to his environment form the basis for the counselee classification discussed in this book.[6] When detected by such means as the counselor has at hand, the psychoneurotic employee should be placed in the care of competent medical authorities. One employee who had made an almost successful attempt at suicide by jumping into a whirling idler pulley was later tested by the best psychiatrist in the state. He was found to be capable of performing simple tasks away from any moving machinery, and a new assignment on the loading dock made a contented workman of him.

Plant counselors should refrain from attempting to probe or to treat cases suspected of being even mildly mentally affected. Diagnosis and care of the mentally ill is a science requiring training, internship, and practice; hence, treatment of the seriously maladjusted will not be discussed beyond recommending early contact with a qualified psychiatrist. Most local psychiatrists and many State Universities can, and will, give the plant counselor specific help in the hospitalization of employees needing mental treatment. The plant physician or nurse may furnish a list of possible sources from which a competent person may select a suitable place for the treatment of an employee with a mental disorder.

[6] Dwight L. Palmer, Eugene R. Purpus, and Lebaron O. Stockford, "Why Workers Quit," *Personnel Journal*, September, 1944, pages 111-119.

The entire population can be divided into groups with special problems of occupational adjustment.   Employed persons in turn may be divided into three groupings: adjusted, unadjusted, and maladjusted.   However, any attempt to classify counselees in terms of rigid, inflexible groups is difficult because conditions involved in individual problems lead to duplication and over-lapping.   Workers who fail to make the necessary occupational, social, and economic adjustments are discussed later in this chapter.   Because the situation confronting veterans will continue to be a lusty adjustment problem for some years to come, it provides an excellent starting point for classifying counselees.

Veterans of Two Wars

All indications point to an early, orderly return of veterans to employment.   The Veterans Administration, the State Employment Services, and the special committees set up by communities, schools, insurance companies, lodges, and dozens of organizations have felt a lively demand for such help as they can furnish the returning G.I. who wants to get re-established.   The Veterans Administration has specialists in many fields to help the veteran obtain information and make the necessary contacts in his re-adjustment to civilian life and employment.   In the larger State Employment Service offices are counselors trained in helping veterans find the paths that lead to satisfactory adjustment in training, job placement, or business.

Possibly, the counselees who will encounter the most difficult readjustment problems in the civilian economy will be those veterans who have traveled the path of the National Youth Administration, the Civilian Conservation Corps, and the military and who are presently entering the labor market for the first time. Their relatively advanced age without a satisfactory private employment work history, and their success in the government fields will tend to make counseling, placement, and adjustment difficult. Low levels of employment entrance, low salaries, and other factors may cause some of these individuals to seek success through opening a business of their own. Like others who choose this path, veterans will find the chances are about 50-50 that they will not succeed during the first two years in their own businesses (according to Department of Commerce figures).

Young People with Limited Skill

The need for counseling is extremely great at this level.[7] While there are fine guidance programs in some of our larger schools, there is still much more to be done than has yet been attempted. The idea of home-room counseling and guidance has grown; paralleling this growth, however, has been the increase in the white-collar fixation. Gradually we are coming to realize that counseling is something more than telling young people what adults think are the niceties of life.

The National Vocational Guidance Association is doing a splendid job in arousing interest in improved guidance programs within the schools of the nation. Among professional journals, first choice of counselors is *Occupations, The Vocational Guidance Magazine*, official organ of The National Vocational Guidance Association, 525 West 120th Street, New York 27, N. Y. The pioneering work of the association stands as a candle lit amid a great darkness.

The United States Department of Labor recognizes the need for assisting young people with their problems. Any well-planned counseling program recognizes the fact that young people are a complex group with wide variation in background and experience. Here are a few categories into which these fledglings seem to fall:

1. Those who have little or no idea of the kind of work they want to do or can do.

---

[7] The effective education of youth should include contact with vocational counselors who are acquainted with the realities of the workaday world. The indispensable nature of this service to the full adjustment of young people is challenging. Howard M. Bell, *Matching Youth and Jobs*, pages 25-26, 29-31, 52-53, 240. Washington: American Council on Education, 1940.

2. Those who have the wrong idea about the field of work they desire to enter.

3. Those who have a need for training and want help in getting started.

4. Those who are, or have been, in jobs unsatisfactory to them and desire assistance in getting into work which better meets their needs.

5. Those who do not know, but are anxious to begin the elementary steps in planning a life's work.

Our young people need help in making an effective adjustment to the world of work. The schools can supply one phase of this program through guidance and counsel. In some instances, State Employment Services are now prepared to offer an improved counseling service to the young people who are seeking suitable job placement. Plant counselors can render a service to the youth of the nation by presenting the true facts about working conditions to young job applicants. Our young people need help, and seasoned industrial counselors have the most valid information. Whenever possible, plant counselors should give thought to the potentialities of the young people in the community and present to them a clear, realistic picture of the employment situation when called upon to appear before school assemblies, civic clubs, or to participate in other community activities.

Older Workers

During periods of surplus labor supply such as we had in the decade from 1930 to 1940, older workers may create a serious economic and social problem, although highly skilled members who have made personal adjustment on the job suffer least under all conditions. Some states have no facilities to provide for the aged workers who are still physically able to support themselves. Other states provide monthly allowances to private individuals who are willing to care for or exploit oldsters, depending upon the circumstances. Light, useful work and the association with other people is desired by many self-respecting, healthy individuals of advanced years. Generally speaking, the higher the skill the greater the possibilities of retention on the job; however, the matter of social adjustment is important in the employment of older workers. World War II was a period in which many older, useful, highly skilled workers returned to much needed employment.

Counselors will find that placing and utilizing these oldsters is a real challenge. Few older employees will ask advice on what to do with an unfaithful wife, but they are likely to want information about Social Security payments. These workmen rendered a great service during the War, and industry might look to that record when skeptics once again point out the possibilities of increased accident rates, higher insurance premiums, increased pension allowances, and similar problems or "dangers" when employing older workers.

Single-skilled Workers

The exigencies of war caused us to train thousands of single-skilled workers, many of whom were thus given their first opportunity to earn living wages. Many of these people are in the labor market to stay. Some of them, unfortunately, find their jobs are now abolished. Retraining will attract certain individuals; others, less stable, will probably refuse retraining and job opportunities below the wage levels of their war-time jobs. The latter often show up in the unemployment statistics even when job opportunities abound. Some will return to their prewar agricultural occupations.

The Physically Handicapped

Problems of the physically handicapped do not frighten us as they once did. Since 1920, funds provided by the National Rehabilitation Act have been used to develop a splendid rehabilitation program which has possibly set a record in practicality and wholesomeness. Various state and local groups also assist the handicapped through their Associations for the Disabled.

The vocational guidance, training, and placement work of the Rehabilitation Service has done much to make industry aware of the potentialities of persons who might otherwise be passed by as unqualified to compete in certain occupations.   Society will ap-·preciate these efforts as thousands of disabled war veterans seek employment.   Hundreds of plants that have done a good or fair job in absorbing crippled civilians with no service record will find it advantageous to absorb many of those men who have given so much for their country.

There are several sound arguments favoring the employment of the handicapped.[8]   Counselors will do well to study these argu-ments, and to advocate the employment of disabled persons for many jobs within the plant.   It might be well for counselors to visit plants employing large numbers of disabled workers.   This type of workman tends to stabilize the work force in a unique manner.   Physically handicapped workers, properly placed, sel-dom leave the plant where they receive initial employment.   Pro-duction record studies made by the War Manpower Commission in Washington, D. C., indicate that careful placement of well-trained, handicapped workers results in satisfactory output with fewer days off the job and fewer gripes.   Rehabilitation is an investment that returns a good profit to the employer; it is worth investigating.

Women

American women might well have been named America's sec-ond secret weapon, next to the Atom bomb.   Unlike the bomb, it was the hiring and not the dropping that caused the furor.   The intense pressure of ever-increasing war production pulled into the labor market thousands of women emotionally unfit for the noisy hum and roar of the production lines.   The average woman quickly adjusted herself to the new industrial surroundings;

---

[8] Ralph W. Emmons, "Program for the Handicapped," *Manpower Review,* Janu-ary, 1944, pages 15-16.

great credit is due womankind for her contribution in the greatest struggle the production line has ever known.

There were certain employees, however, who needed help. Vocational Training Schools had helped some adjust gradually to the surroundings and tempo of factory work, but counselors were needed to assist several man-dominated industries in overcoming certain situations that the influx of women had brought. Few men admit understanding a wife; can they be expected to understand several hundred women?

While the presence of certain types of women may create a problem, all women in industry are not considered special counseling problems. Careful selection, realistic training, adequate induction, specific orientation, and well-timed follow-up will do much to dispel the notion that women require special treatment in industrial plants.

Maladjusted Workers

Maladjusted workers are those who have not successfully made the necessary adjustment to the occupation in which they find themselves. If the worker can be assisted in identifying the cause of his failure to become adjusted, and the obstacles standing between adjustment and the worker can be removed, the counselor has done a good job of salvaging a fellow human being. Frequently, however, failure to make adjustment has its foundation in the personality of the worker. If the task assigned brings about a nervous condition in the employee which may end in a mental crack-up, consideration should be given promptly to a more suitable job assignment. On the other hand, it takes subtle persuasion to get an employee to face reality, stand firm, and see his problem through to the finish. Many workers, capable of performing excellently in another field of work, will, because of fear, refuse to advance or move into jobs that better suit their capacities. On the other hand, strong-minded individuals with little talent frequently undertake tasks that make them nervous, irritable, and difficult to associate with on the job.

There are many reasons for occupational maladjustment. Counselors, by using testing and interviewing techniques, can probe for the causes involved, and render service to the worker and management alike in exposing the causes of difficulty.[9] Outmoded hiring methods that bring together all workers to compete on equal footing regardless of their ability, preparation, or experience makes for many maladjustments. Not all workers fit into the pattern set by industry, nor are alternate jobs the answer to all maladjustments.

The Occupationally Unadjusted

Individuals who have never been gainfully employed are considered occupationally unadjusted. Workers who have been successful in one line but who have a desire to try their hand at something else may be considered unadjusted. There are many other workers who have failed to make the necessary adjustment to specific elements in their environment. The term *unadjusted* means that the individual does not feel that what he is doing satisfies him enough to make continuance in that occupation worth the necessary effort. Consequently, the individual continues to seek something which he feels will suit him better or satisfy him more deeply.

The Economically Unadjusted

The term *maladjusted* is possibly more descriptive of the so-called economically unadjusted individual. We are thinking of the individual who has failed to make the necessary adjustments in his life that will place him in balance with his earning power. Such workers frequently have legal problems which take them from the plant. Their time is spent in finding signers and co-signers for notes—not on work production. Worry over personal

---

[9] Much valuable information about employees has been gained through the use of exit interviews. The technique of exit interviewing is described by the War Department, Civilian Relations Branch in an article entitled "Mechanics of the Exit Interview," *Personnel,* January, 1944, pages 231-239. New York: American Management Association.

matters is not conducive to high morale.[10]   In general, the unadjusted employees in a plant can create problems that are hard
to cope with because these individuals seldom come to the counselor for help.   Strangely enough, these workers infrequently use
the Credit Union or other plant loan facilities; usually, they have
spent beyond a wise credit limit and can raise money only at rates
of interest far beyond their power to repay.

The Socially Unadjusted

Extreme sensitivity resulting from a feeling of not "belonging"
frequently marks the socially unadjusted.   Poor induction and
orientation practices may aggravate the condition when sensitive
individuals enter new employment.   Foremen who do not make
clear-cut assignments sometimes cause unstable workers to
"crack-up" under the strain of not knowing whether their work
is satisfactory or not.   Plant cliques exert a pressure that eventually causes a sensitive worker to "blow his top" when the latter
gets too much steam pent up.

Supervision plays an important part in the social adjustment of
the worker to the plant.   Where social maladjustment occurs,
the problem is usually more serious.   Prompt action must be
taken against sex offenders or complete demoralization of the
working force may result.   The supervisory load should be ex-
amined promptly if there is time in a department for such behavior during the working day.   Horseplay, another type of social
maladjustment that usually results in industrial accidents, may be
traced to a laxity on the part of foremen and supervisors, or to
an overloaded supervisory staff.

Questions

1. Define counseling.
2. From what sources are counselees referred?

---

[10] Personal problems of a financial or social nature arising outside the plant affect
production.   For a discussion of *worry* as it relates to industrial productivity see
"Helping the Worried Worker," *Personnel,* September, 1944, pages 84-90.   New
York: American Management Association.

3. What are the important factors in Mike Malloy's situation?   Draw a chart showing the contacts made by the counselor.

4. If you would place the counselor elsewhere in the pattern, justify your position.

5. Is it desirable to have satisfied workers?   Discuss.

6. What are some of the evidences of worker dissatisfaction?

7. Can we classify counselees?   If so, how?   If not, why?

8. What government agency is conducting an extensive counseling program for adults?   Why is it needed?

9. Into what categories may one classify young people who need counseling?

10. Discuss the maladjusted worker.   How does he compare or contrast with the occupationally unadjusted?   The economically unadjusted?   The socially unadjusted?

Bibliography

Hoppock, R., *Job Satisfaction, Part I*.   New York: Harper & Brothers, 1935.

Houser, J. D., *What People Want from Business*.   New York: McGraw-Hill Book Company, 1938.

Roethlisberger, F. J., *Management and Morale, Part I*.   Boston: Harvard University Press, 1946.

Super, Donald E., *The Dynamics of Vocational Adjustment*, Chapter XV.   New York: Harper & Brothers, 1942.

Counseling to Meet a Need   2

GOOD morale among employees is not an industrial happen-stance; it is something that must be developed, fostered, and maintained. Morale stems from a feeling of mutual respect between workers and all levels of supervision. This feeling reaches its height when employees sense that management has a warm, friendly attitude towards them. Morale reaches its lowest point when employees sense an ill-timed or over-zealous paternalism on the part of management. In the past, management has too frequently manifested greater concern over materials, machinery, and the production of the plant than for the thoughts, feelings, and contentions of its workers. Effectively functioning personnel departments will bring about a consensus that management *does* have a genuine interest in the welfare of its employees. Counselors can and should strengthen this feeling among employees.

The matter of developing good-will requires teamwork. A personnel department and its counseling staff do not function as independent ambassadors of good-will at the expense of those responsible for meeting production schedules. All production supervisors perform some personnel functions, and must assume responsibility for properly carrying out policies of the company. The personnel department should assist the supervisory staff in its problems without overstepping established plant lines of authority. Through such joint effort, plant employees should benefit from better occupational adjustment and improved worker morale.

Worker dissatisfaction seems chronic in some plants; in others, pleasant working conditions constantly prevail. Finding the cause of worker dissatisfaction is not a simple matter of reading the plant bulletin board for "gripes." It is necessary to know a plant intimately to identify all the problems that assert themselves in poor workmanship, low morale, and flagging production. The first step in overcoming the ills of an ailing plant is to identify some of the common problems.

In-plant Problems

Inadequate Induction

Inadequate induction increases the turnover rate of new employees. If workers are not staying long enough to pay the cost of breaking-in, a review of the induction practices is in order. Induction should be thought of as the *introduction* of the new worker *to the plant, to the department* and *to the job*. Induction is considered to be general enough in nature to be conducted by the personnel department. Employee orientation, on the other hand, is specific and should be handled by the supervisor.[1] Failure to understand plant policies, practices, rules, and regulations leads to misunderstanding and dissatisfaction. A new worker who feels he has started off on the wrong foot is likely to quit rather than stick it out. Leaving the plant under these conditions gives human beings one of those rare opportunities to flee rather than to stay and face the music. Plant safety rules, for example, are important enough to justify an induction plan. Reduced premiums on compensation policies resulting from a decrease in the accident rate would easily pay the over-all cost of induction in all but the safest plants.

Induction has the advantages of getting the worker and the management together on common ground before the attitude of the worker has crystallized. Properly timed induction gives new employees a sense of orderliness that is important. Delay in informing workers of accepted plant policies, practices, and customs may cause resentment if presented after some minor infraction of

---

[1] There are those who do not agree with the authors on this point. "Introducing the New Employee to the Job," *Personnel,* July, 1943, pages 15-22. New York: American Management Association.

the rules has occurred. The feeling thus created may be sufficiently strong to cause the worker to quit immediately. A good induction program can be a safety safeguard and the source of satisfaction to both employees and management.

Poor Orientation

Poor orientation should not be confused with inadequate induction. Orientation involves *early adjustment to a specific job.* The foreman, lead man, or some designated worker should help the new employee chart his course. Workers transferred to new assignments should be oriented in order to speed up the period of adjustment and reduce to a minimum the period of lowered production.

Orientation may be described as "getting of one's bearings on the job." Questions typical of the orientation period include: To whom do I go for help? What is the simplest, most direct method of performing this task? How many pieces shall I make? A host of answers to anticipated questions supplied by the person responsible for the orientation procedure should clarify many points which puzzle the worker attempting to become adjusted to a new job. If occupational adjustment is a desired goal, then orientation should be put into effect along with an adequate induction program. In the literature of counseling, the words induction and orientation are frequently used synonymously. The attempt has been made to distinguish between induction and orientation functions.[2] *Induction introduces the worker to the plant and the department; orientation adjusts the worker to the job and the operation.*

Poor Physical Environment

Poor physical environment may cost an employer more in lost time than would the expense of bringing conditions up to standard.

---

[2] The word *orientation* is used in the broad sense of the term in the following pamphlet: "Orienting the New Worker," Policyholders Service Bureau, Metropolitan Life Insurance Company, New York, 1944.

Extremes in cold, heat, moisture, and dryness have their effect upon production. Not all conditions of this kind can be overcome completely. Certain types of production require that operations be performed under conditions unfavorable to optimum human comfort. The wood room in a paper mill, the roundhouse in a railroad shop and the wash rack in a garage are typical locations where extremes of temperature, moisture, gas, and other unpleasant working conditions prevail. The use of exhaust fans, heating units, self-closing doors, and other modern devices will do much to keep worker morale at a high level. Wherever possible, a considerate attitude toward worker comfort, coupled with improvement in production methods, can achieve much in improving plant conditions.

Counselors should be alert to suggestions from employees for the correction of those conditions which tend to damage morale and hinder rapid occupational adjustment: poor lighting reduces maximum output, and poor ventilation induces fatigue. Such inadequacies may also be spotted by the counselor while passing through the plant. Dust and dirt may be similarly detected. Individual masks and other safeguards may serve as a temporary means of alleviating these discomforts. A campaign for permanent improvements should be tactfully carried on by the personnel department, its counselor, and the safety engineer.

An Absence of Approbation

Among workers an absence of approbation ranks high as the cause for dissatisfaction. Failure to give credit when due tends to make work humdrum and discouraging: demoralizing workers, hampering production, and increasing labor turnover. It may lead to group action on the part of workers desirous of bringing about a crisis; such conditions often result in serious labor trouble. Good working relationships between worker and foreman are extremely important to management. Psychology and sociology have contributed much by furnishing an understanding of the forces that motivate individuals and groups.[3] The judicious use of approbation gives the foreman one of mankind's strongest motivating forces. Individuals have a strong desire for praise. Receipt of well-deserved praise gives workers the inner strength to move forward to new heights of attainment. Those failing to receive approbation when it is due feel a letdown which is soon reflected in the quality and quantity of output.

The counselor is in a strategic position to use approbation to advantage. He should point out its merits to foremen and others who deal with human relations problems. Foremen frequently need to be reminded that one word of praise from a well-liked individual has more motivating power than a thousand cusswords from a chronic griper.

Lack of Incentives

The lack of incentives frequently affects workers adversely. Incentives may include money, time off, or approbation. Workers seem to strive for all three. Plants that fail to use money to best advantage as an incentive find it increasingly difficult to meet competition. Profit sharing, bonus payment plans for predetermined levels of production, and piece rates are incentive plans in common use. Money, however, is not the only thing that men work for. Thousands of workers accept employment as necessary to survival. Daily, these employees seek the inner gratification that comes from pleasant association with fellow workers, genuine approbation from respected foremen, and the satisfaction that comes from being a member of a going concern. Plants that make no provision for satisfying some of these motivating urges fail to make the best possible use of the available manpower in the organization.

A few employers with an eye to the future are thinking of in-

[3] For a clear statement of the application of the findings in these two fields to the work situation, see: Ellis C. Maxcy, "Understanding People in Work Relationships," *Personnel,* May, 1942, pages 371-376. New York: American Management Association.

centives that will dispel the fear of insecurity felt by many employees. Annual wages, vacations with pay, and pay envelopes that fluctuate in size with commodity prices challenge the counselor to become better informed about factors that make men happy in their work. Some people need the feeling of social prestige that certain jobs give them, while others feel the need for greater security.

Security programs for employees have moved forward so rapidly in the past two decades that some managers are incapable of explaining to workers the benefits to be derived from various paycheck deductions. Clear-cut explanations and graphic aids worked out by an intelligent counselor will assist in keeping workers informed and satisfied. Resentment and distrust grow in the minds of workers who are "kept in the dark." Not all employees have the time and the ability to read and interpret lengthy statements filled with superlatives. Periodicals, newsletters, and a well-illustrated plant magazine will do much to eliminate prejudices, if presented in a style that attracts and holds reader interest.[4] A constant educational campaign is needed to keep workers abreast of what is happening to their pay checks. When a new deduction occurs, the little wife at home sees only the smaller pay check. She will not blame the management if she knows why the deduction is being made. Do you wonder that not all counseling problems are in-plant?

Out-plant Problems

The out-plant problems which affect workers may be divided into three main groups: social, economic, and obligatory.

Social Problems

Workers with an above-average amount of spare time frequently engage in certain activities "on the side" that net them

---

[4] For an interesting discussion of in-plant morale building methods read: Meyer Brown, M.D., Ph.D., *Morale in Industry as Seen by a Neuropsychiatrist*, pages 21-29. Chicago: Industrial Welfare Department, Zurich Insurance Companies.

additional cash. Unions represented by the sideline occupation have a way of asking the full-time employer to discipline
the "shade tree" mechanic. One such case involved a man who
painted houses as a sideline. Union painters appealed to the
full-time employer to make the man cease his painting activity
under the penalty of being fired if he refused to agree. Many
license laws are enacted to prevent all but the "qualified" from
plying a trade. The counselor needs to know what to do when

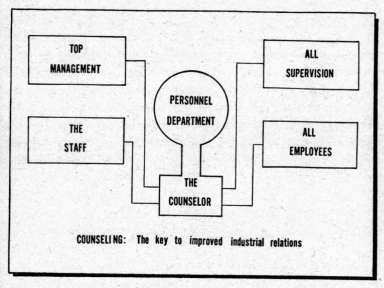

COUNSELING: The key to improved industrial relations

THE STRATEGIC POSITION OF THE COUNSELOR MAKES IT POSSIBLE FOR HIM TO
FUNCTION AS THE KEY TO SUCCESSFUL INDUSTRIAL RELATIONS.

injuries occur in these sideline jobs, and what to say when the
plant nurse is asked to treat such injuries. Who pays the compensation if an infection sets in after such treatment?—the
worker may ask. As manifold as the related problems seem to
be, they do not begin to cover the leisure time activities of workers. Problems that reach the counselor include the broken home,
the other woman, the drunkard, the squanderer, and many others.
The counselor must have a solution for the woman who stays

home to watch her husband—"so he doesn't head for that other woman's house again." He must know what to do about the fellow who fails to show up, but who calls up from Joe's Bar to tell the boss he has had too many beers and can't make it in time for the midnight shift. It would be well to have a plan of action for the fellow who made it past the plant guard safely, but who is now too drunk and sleepy to carry on at his machine.

Counselors know that the employee who leads a church or school group seldom gets into difficulties of a social nature. Likewise, the man who is selected as the best player on the bowling team, or elected to an important post in his lodge, or who leads a group of Scouts in the community, rarely figures in situations involving social problems.[5] There is a need to encourage wholesome social activity that will occupy more fully the increasing leisure time available to employees now that shorter working hours are commonplace. Such activity can be encouraged through the organization of plant bands, bowling teams, training programs, athletic councils, and dozens of other activities that are run *by* and *for* workers.

Economic Problems

Economic problems of a wide variety affect the workers of this nation. Many of the problems stem from over-spending or the abuse of credit privileges. Some plants have rules that affect the status of a worker garnisheed a given number of times. It is not unusual for a young worker employed only a few days to seek funds, signers for a note, an advance in salary, or a loan from the boss to buy a good used convertible car he saw on the market last week. When pressed for a reason for buying such an expensive model, he is likely to tell you that he has it on good authority

---

[5] As long as our behavior conforms to the prescribed pattern set up by those around us, we are usually considered social or socialized. A discussion of the importance of customs in everyday behavior is given by F. J. Roethlisberger in a chapter entitled "The Social Structure of Industry," from *Management and Morale*. Cambridge: Harvard University Press, 1946.

that this particular car once belonged to the King of Siam—"and brother, it has all the gadgets in the world on it."

Credit Unions have been of great help to thousands of workers who might otherwise be paying excessive rates of interest to loan sharks; local bankers have also furnished sound financial aid to reliable workmen. The co-operative aspects of the Credit Union give the workers some concept of organization and experience in finance. The counselor would do well to take a wholesome attitude toward the Credit Union idea and do all in his power to foster the idea among plant employees. Besides tiding an individual over a thin spot, the Union pays a premium to the employee who has money to place on loan with the Credit Union.

The welfare activities of the plant need the close co-operation of the counselor. Accidents, fires, a death, and other misfortunes strike workers from time to time. Some plants have special funds from which workers may borrow without paying interest. A shelter for a burned-out, homeless family, a holiday basket for an injured worker, a casket for a lost child, all are part of the warm, friendly spirit which can radiate from an employer with a heart— and a counselor with vision.

Obligatory Problems

The complexities of our society have placed upon all of us certain obligations which require unavoidable absences from work. One must appear in person to get a Social Security account number. Licenses of various kinds must be applied for personally; one cannot send a proxy to pass a driver's license test. Even minor law violations usually require an employee's appearance in court. These and other transactions require that the person involved be at a given location at a specific time. A pretty definite pattern of waiving attendance at work for such genuinely citizen-like duties as voting and jury sitting has been worked out. The petty summons also must always be met *in person*. To the counselor falls the task of checking, evaluating, and recording absences from the plant for obligatory reasons.

Kinds of Counseling

The increasing complexity of our daily living strengthens the desire for suggestions that will clarify our problems. Adults are turning to a variety of sources for counsel. Friends, neighbors, and acquaintances offer opinions, and doctors, lawyers, and ministers furnish professional advice on more serious problems. The sincere, puzzled individual is seeking sage advice in the hope that his difficulties will be ironed out and a more satisfactory way of living found. This desire for outside help has grown to a point where radio stations, magazines, and newspapers all present counseling advice of one kind or another. A more personal service is being offered by banks, business houses and public utilities to their customers. An alarming number of shingles are being hung out by pseudo-psychologists and psychoanalysts.

As the matter now stands, there are three distinct kinds of counseling: (1) Privateer, (2) Trained Psychiatrist, and (3) Personnel Counselor. The privateer entered the field chiefly for the cash that can be earned quickly; his motto is "You pays your money and you takes what you get." A clear picture of their actions is presented by Miss Steiner in her book *Where Do People Take Their Troubles?* [6]

The trained psychiatrist renders a genuine service to those needing help with serious mental troubles. Maladjusted and seriously unadjusted individuals should have the advice and counsel of these trained and experienced doctors who understand clinical procedures and case work. Every unadjusted plant worker does not need such service, and most workmen would cease being seen in the presence of a counselor if they felt that it would label them a "case." Certain groups feel that the plant counselor should be trained in psychology beyond classroom work,[7] but this theory is open to debate. The plant counselor

---

[6] Lee R. Steiner, *Where Do People Take Their Troubles?* Boston: Houghton Mifflin Company, 1945.

[7] For the extremes in counselor requirements see the references below. The authors recognize the difference in the situations involved. A comparison is not

does not need to be a trained psychologist, and he most certainly
need not be a graduate psychiatrist.

Plant counselors can render useful free services to employees in
helping them to resolve their in-plant and out-plant problems.
These counselors do not charge fees for the services they render.
They do not think of those seeking their advice as *cases;* rather,
they think of workers as *individuals*. The plant counselor helps
the individual to define his problem, get the facts, and then he assists the individual in making a wise decision of his own.

We have delayed overlong needed legislation to control the
privateer in the counseling field. Laws will probably be enacted
to curb all but the legitimate practitioners when the public
becomes sufficiently aroused to the thorough "cleaning" these
privateers are giving them. Individuals who can afford it would
do well to take their problems to the family physician, the minister, a reputable psychologist, or a psychiatrist. A psychologist
recommended by one's personal physician is a safe choice. The
competent plant counselor will help the individual to help himself.
This tends to strengthen the individual rather than to make him
feel he must return time after time for a detailed plan when in
doubt or in trouble.

Counseling to Close the Foreman-Personnel Department Gap

The owner and master of the shop in early times hired, trained,
and elevated to journeymanship promising young workers. In
those days, the burden of selecting, outfitting, orienting, up-grad-
ing, and counseling rested upon the employer-owner. Expansion
of the one-man business resulted in the hiring of an overseer.

fair, but the divergence is interesting. *The Employee Counselor in Industry,* pages
5-6. New York: Policyholders Service Bureau, Metropolitan Life Insurance Company. Franklin J. Keller and Morris S. Viteles, *Vocational Guidance Throughout
the World,* pages 44-49, 60-61. New York: W. W. Norton and Company, Inc.,
1937. *The Training of Vocational Counselors,* 77 pages, Bureau of Training, Department of Labor. Washington: Superintendent of Documents, Government
Printing Office, 1944.

This division of the management function resulted in the owner continuing to select and employ, while the overseer took over the training and the imparting of skills. As industries have grown, further division of work has occurred.

In modern plants, personnel departments perform the activities which were formerly the responsibilities of the foreman and the owner. Delegation of these duties to a third party has created a gap in the relationship between the foreman and the personnel department. The complexities of worker problems, plus certain legislative prohibitions like those contained in the Wagner Act, as well as certain liberties contained in the recently enacted Taft-Hartley Bill, none of which are altogether clear to foremen, have made an even wider gap between the foreman and his men. The tendency recently has been to relieve the foreman of all but the most rudimentary human relations problems. As a result, if the foreman meets production schedules and gets along well with his men, management is well pleased.

We are not to decide here whether stripping the foreman of many of his former personnel responsibilities is good or bad. Experiences of individual plants vary. One thing is certain, "before and after" conditions furnish the evidence as to the wisdom of revising foremen's duties and responsibilities. The human relations situation is growing more complex, and industrial processes are becoming more intricate. Better-trained foremen and further division of the supervisory function are two obvious solutions. Both have been evident in recent years.

Personnel departments have been assuming responsibility for an increasing number of employees' human relations problems. Today, the personnel department contacts the worker through the processes of application-taking, selection, induction, training, transfers, morale building programs, accepting suggestions, counseling, disciplining, and so on. Certain of the activities just listed could best be performed on the shop floor instead of handling them in a central office. Proof of this may be gained by

reviewing what made a successful foreman in former years.   The
supervisor who knew his men, treated them as individuals, counseled with them freely, and worked with them fairly seldom
needed help from outside the department.   Foremen who recognize this fact can hardly be blamed for feeling resentful or cool
toward personnel departments; and so the gap widens unless someone in authority has the ability to reconcile the entire situation.

Counselors should maintain private offices for conference work,
but should move freely about the plant to contact foremen and
workers.   The counselor's degree of success may be evaluated
in terms of how well the gap between the foreman and the personnel department is bridged.   When the counselor visits the production floors, minor problems can be settled on the spot.   Intricate
problems should be settled in the privacy of the counselor's office
after an understanding has been reached between counselor and
foreman.   The "understanding" referred to at this point does not
necessarily involve the foreman's knowing what the worker's
problem encompasses, but there must be *no misunderstanding
between the counselor and the foreman over the "mechanics" of
helping the worker with his problem*.   The liaison work of the
counselor can improve employee morale and bring the foreman
and the personnel department much closer together.

Activities That Meet a Need

The question is frequently raised—What are the activities that
a counselor may consider within his sphere of influence?   As
mentioned on page 34, some of the activities which formerly de-
volved upon the foreman have now become complex enough to
merit the attention of a specialist.   The authors, having analyzed
counselor duties in a variety of plants, suggest the following three-
word description of counselor duties: co-ordination, consultation,
and confabulation.   While these words pretty well cover the nature of the counseling job, they do not indicate where the three

C's may be practiced.   Activities in which the counselor can meet a need and can render a service include the following:

Health and Safety	Recreational Activities
Morale and Worker Interest	Canteens and Cafeterias
Loans and Financial Help	Home Visits
Credit Unions	Transportation
Old Age Benefits	Welfare
Unemployment Compensation	Social Problems
Insurance Provisions	Economic Problems
Wage or Salary Deductions	Adjustment Problems

The alert plant counselor may discover additional fields where he may render service, too.   The counselor should serve as a TROUBLE SHOOTER for all levels of supervision and management. What is more important, he can and should prevent many problems from arising.

Co-ordination

Elimination of duplicated effort is an important phase of the counselor's work.   Through his close contact with employees, the counselor can obtain, and present to those responsible for policy-making, a point of view that reflects the thinking of the work force.   When sufficient material has been gathered to indicate trends, it should result in the adoption, modification, and incorporation of practices and policies that tend to improve the morale of the work force.

Feelings, sentiments, opinions, and reactions must be gathered carefully on a long-range basis to be of value in policy-making. The experienced counselor realizes that jumping to conclusions is a poor technique and that continuance of such practice will get him into trouble.   Winning acceptance is not always difficult if one carefully interprets the various opinions of those involved, and gears his proposition accordingly.   Policies and practices that win acceptance without interrupting production reflect the quality of co-ordination activities of the counselor who at all times has his hand on the pulse of the work force.

Consultation

The counselor provides a friendly ear that lets the worker get all problems "off his chest."   To avoid misunderstandings, supervisors and foremen should be fully informed of these meetings.

Rodney deSARRO

THE SATURDAY
EVENING POST

"For a nickel, you can tell her all your troubles
and she'll nod sympathetically."

Courtesy of The Curtis Publishing Company.

CONSULTATION IS NOT INTENDED AS A DEVICE TO "PUT THE
COUNSELOR ON THE SPOT."

The counselor should avoid making decisions that lead foremen to feel that they are being short-circuited or by-passed by the counselor. This friendly listening-post service promotes the feeling among employees that management has an interest in their problems. Consultation builds morale—creates good-will—by relieving pent-up tensions and smoothing the "troubled waters" for the plant. When the interview is unhurried, and the counselor considerate, the employee gets a sense of great satisfaction from the experience.

There are certain outcomes in the interview which have a wholesome effect.   The telling process relieves accumulated tension and pressure, gets real or imagined grievances out in the open, gives the employee a new sense of importance through the feeling that management is interested in him as an individual, and gives the employee an opportunity to make a decision based upon the facts in the situation.   The mere recitation of details gets problems into their proper perspective, often reduces their magnitude to zero, and does much towards giving the individual a feeling that he has secured satisfaction.

Consultation is not intended as a device to put the counselor on the spot.   If a genuine problem confronts the worker, the counselor, through the use of a definite technique to be described in Chapter 13, helps the worker to help himself. The counselor does not come forth with some predetermined solution to the problem, nor should he do the work involved in making the decision as to what should be done.   The wise counselor will strengthen every counselee with each contact.   To weaken the counselee by doing his work in solving a problem also undermines the counselor's position in the personnel department structure.   A complete breakdown comes when the counselor spends *all* his time chasing trouble and has no time for the preventive activities of his job.

Confabulation

Confabulation is the informal conversation between worker and counselor as the latter visits throughout the plant. Topics may vary—passing the time of the day, getting details of some worker's fishing trip, or congratulating a new father.   Confabulation is a part of the goodwill-building so necessary to a successful counseling program. The warmth radiated by the counselor during these meetings may be the making or breaking point in his career. Many jobs have a warming-up or preliminary period; confabulation is one such period in counseling. Employees will not gravitate to a person they do not trust, respect, or admire; confabulation helps to create these attitudes.

Counselors cannot always steer a course pleasant to the counselee in the private consultation; facing facts and meeting issues realistically is sometimes disagreeable business. In confabulation, every day can be bright, every face a mirror for your smile. How well this personal selling is done will be reflected in the demands for your services as a counselor.

Some Functioning Programs

The Metropolitan Life Insurance Company and R. H. Macy & Company were pioneers in the counseling movement. Government agencies began developing counseling services about 1933, when the New Deal got under way. One outstanding governmental program started in 1938 was that of the Social Security Board.

Wartime activity and a tight labor market brought into being many programs designed to improve employee morale and reduce turnover. A few programs, the result of accelerated wartime growth, are best classified as "fly by night." These programs frequently were designed to meet the most serious problems of crowded war plants. The term applies because with a reduction of the work force and a subsequent easing of worker problems, the counseling function was eliminated. Human relations problems exist wherever a group is assembled for work or other reasons. Ending of the wartime pressure for production somewhat reduced workers' problems, but it did not eliminate them. It takes time to prove the quality of a counseling program.

In reading the literature of counseling, one finds repeated frequently the names of certain plants whose counseling systems have stood the acid test of time. The six programs described are especially well known.

Metropolitan Life Insurance Company

In 1922, the Metropolitan Life Insurance Company recognized the need for a service to supervisors and employees which would deal with mental as well as physical upsets or disorders.[8] A psychiatrist was employed to deal with minor mental disturbances and to prevent such conditions from arising. This consultation service has developed into a counseling program. It is the earliest recorded program of its kind from which we can get reliable information as to the value and outcomes of such a service. One proof of its worth is the fact that the program is still operating today.

R. H. Macy & Company

The next oldest successful program of which there is a record is the one established by R. H. Macy & Company in 1925.[9] Through what was termed a mental hygiene program, management was brought to realize that the *whole person*, adjusted, unadjusted, or maladjusted, reports to work. His or her worries and personal problems definitely affect job adjustment and productivity. Their research reports show that the social reactions during working hours have a direct connection with the quality and quantity of work.

Western Electric Hawthorne Plant Experiment

Much has been written about the research carried on in 1927 and subsequent years at the Western Electric Company's Hawthorne Plant. One interesting fact is that both the management

---

[8] Lydia G. Giberson, "Emotional First-Aid Stations in Industry," *Personnel,* August, 1939, pages 1-15. New York: American Management Association.

[9] For a discussion of medicine at work in industry see: V. V. Anderson, M.D., "Psychiatry in Industry," *Preventive Management,* pages 53-90. B. C. Forbes Co., 1931.

and organized labor at Hawthorne have agreed that the counseling program is a sound one and highly important in maintaining good management-employee relations.

The rapidity with which counseling programs spread during the period of World War II led many to believe it would pass from the personnel picture as rapidly. Those who see value in the human relations aspects of the service are convinced that counseling in some form will continue. Workers' problems, they reason, are growing increasingly complex.[10] In the Hawthorne Plant experiment favorable treatment of employees, which made them feel that they were being especially well-treated and created a sense of satisfaction, proved to be the most effective motivation for obtaining quantity and quality production. The management provided an opportunity for the employees to "tell their side of the story" by discussing personal reactions and interests, and demonstrated a genuine interest in what the employees said. The private interview was the technique used, and much time and attention was devoted to *how* to conduct an interview. By developing effective interviewing techniques, management learned much of the sentiments and feelings of their employees.[11] The research counselors discovered that, as in the R. H. Macy program, the feeling and attitudes of employees affected productivity.

Social Security Board

In 1938, the Social Security Board—now a part of the Federal Security Agency—initiated a counseling program under the guidance and leadership of Margaret E. Barron. The program, a function of the F.S.A. personnel department, is described as "a

---

[10] Speculation along this line is carried further by: Burleigh B. Gardner, "Employee Counseling in Private Industry," *Public Personnel Review,* January, 1945, pages 6-8. Chicago: Civil Service Assembly. F. J. Roethlisberger and William J. Dickson, *Management and the Worker.* Cambridge: Harvard University Press, 1943.

[11] No discussion of employee reaction would be complete without recognition of the Goodyear Aircraft program. This topic is interestingly covered by: S. E. Fuller, "Goodyear Aircraft Employee Counseling," *Personnel Journal,* October, 1944, pages 145-153.

combination of government personnel work, guidance, psychiatric and social case work and recreational work, plus certain other activities which do not fall into clearly defined categories." [12] Before World War II, the program was considered successful by those interested in counseling as a part of personnel work.   During the war period influx of government workers to Washington, this program, because of its early establishment, was able to render an even greater service to workers needing housing, transportation, and other assistance.

The War Department and the Navy Department

The War Department, one of the largest employers in the world, has described counseling functions in the following manner:

> Counseling services aim to help the employee who has individual problems pertaining to his personal well-being or to his employment.   If a problem arises which an employee cannot handle by himself, he needs to know that he can go to some one person and get help.   The first person he turns to is the supervisor, especially if the difficulty is related directly to the job.   But many times the matter has to do with factors the supervisor has no time to deal with and on which he has no information.   Moreover, certain difficulties arise on the job which the employee will not discuss with the supervisor, such as trouble with other employees, some kinds of job complaints, and unsatisfactory relationships with the supervisor.   The employee counselor, provided by management to assist employees and thereby to help the supervisors maintain a stable, efficient working force is in possession of information and knowledge which he can bring to bear on the solution of individual problems.
>
> An employee counselor usually performs the following functions:
>> (1) Assists the employee in orienting himself to his work and to his associates.

---

[12] Margaret E. Barron, "Employee Counseling in a Federal Agency," *Personnel Administration,* March, 1942, page 6.   Washington: Society for Personnel Administration.

(2) Assists the employee in working out satisfactory living arrangements.

(3) Observes attitudes and reactions of the employee which prevent him from doing his best work, and helps workers to develop better conduct and attitudes on the job.

(4) Identifies problems of individual employees which need special attention and makes referrals to proper agencies.

(5) Discovers conditions within the work situation which may prevent the employee from giving his best performance and recommends remedies.

(6) Aids supervisors in establishing harmonious, cooperative, and understanding relationships with their employees.

(7) Assists in interpreting management policies and practices for employees and in turn reflects to managing officials the reactions of employees to these policies and practices.[13]

The National Vocational Guidance Association

In 1913, the National Vocational Guidance Association[14] was founded to improve the quality of work done by persons charged with the responsibility of giving occupational information and guidance service. Their present program, which emphasizes counseling for satisfactory job placement, includes these activities:

(1) furnishing occupational or vocational information

(2) assisting with an analysis of the individual's assets and liabilities

(3) offering counseling and help in matching job requirements to the information listed during the individual analysis

(4) making suggestions as to preparation necessary for successful employment

(5) assisting, directly or indirectly, in placing individuals

(6) offering assistance in making adjustment to the job

(7) providing a research service to develop and test techniques,

---

[13] "Personnel Counseling," Civilian Personnel Pamphlet No. 1, War Department. Washington: United States Government Printing Office, 1943.

[14] National Vocational Guidance Association, Inc., publishers of the magazine *Occupations*. Headquarters, 82 Beaver Street, New York 5, N. Y.

devices, and methods for effective guidance and counseling procedures.

Flexibility in Newer Programs

Department stores, banks, and public utilities have for some years past carried on effective customer-service organizations. The usual technique has been to employ a well-qualified person to render necessary services of a public relations nature. Sometimes the service has been an information booth, sometimes a demonstration program; always, however, assistance, advice, and counsel is given those who ask for it. Customer service has appealed to the public, and today the demand is great for competent individuals to perform this work. Nearly all banks have set up programs to advise veterans on such subjects as their rights under the G.I. Bill of Rights: information on loans, extension of credit, and the financing of various undertakings.

Insurance companies and public utilities, alert to the value of counseling programs for veterans, were among the first to establish such services. The scope of their counseling activity is limited only by the problems presented and the ability of the counselor. One familiar service of the public utilities is the home demonstration program available to every person who makes a purchase. Free information is also furnished those who visit the local offices of their utilities. Demand for advice is assuredly on the increase. It is therefore logical to assume that counseling and related services will continue to expand. This growth may be limited, however, by an inadequate supply of counselors and advisers capable of meeting the many problems presented by an eager public. While there is a shortage of thoroughly skilled counselors, there is no lack of individuals *purporting* to know the techniques of counseling.

These nonindustrial counseling programs are somewhat similar to public relations work but are run on a more flexible basis than the services that industry has set up for its workers. As a result, the training of counselors is more complex. Certain institutions

of higher learning, Ohio State University, for example, are prepared to meet the challenge, but many counselors will have to
content themselves with courses in the field of personnel management and educational and vocational guidance. Customer counseling may eventually be recognized as a legitimate field and
specific training provided for specialists in the field.[15]

Counseling for business establishments is no longer limited to
giving sales advice; it now encompasses a multiplicity of subjects.

Questions

1. What is management's attitude toward employees as illustrated in
   the report on research programs conducted by the Western Electric
   Company, Hawthorne Works, Chicago, Illinois?
2. List and discuss In-plant problems that confront employees and
   affect management.
3. What is the difference between induction and orientation?
4. What are considered to be Out-plant problems?
5. Is there "privateering" in the field of counseling?   Discuss.
6. Are foremen and supervisors always prepared to handle the human
   relations problems of employees?   If not, where does the counselor
   fit in?
7. List ten activities performed by counselors.
8. What are the "3 C's of Counseling"?
9. Name and discuss three counseling programs.   Include one pioneer
   program.
10. Discuss the reasons for flexibility in the newer programs.

Bibliography

Barron, Margaret E., "Employee Counseling in a Federal Agency," *Personnel Administration,* March, 1942. Washington: Society for
Personnel Administration.

Bergen, H. B., "Finding Out What Employees Are Thinking," *The Conference Board Management Record.* Washington: United States
Government Printing Office, 1939.

---

[15] For a comprehensive program and list of co-operating agencies, corporations,
and associations read the "Peoria Plan for Human Rehabilitation," The Peoria
Plan, 415 Liberty Street, Peoria 2, Ill., 1943. Revised April, 1944.

Maier, Norman R. F., *Psychology in Industry,* pages 410-415.   Boston: Houghton Mifflin Company, 1946.

Roethlisberger, F. J., and Dickson, William J., *Management and the Worker.*   Boston: Harvard University Press, 1943.

"Personnel Counseling," Civilian Personnel Pamphlet No. 1, War Department.   Washington: United States Government Printing Office, 1943.

Counseling Rehabilitants   3

PLANT counselors are frequently called upon to work with counselors from various public agencies. Good working relationships among these counselors depend largely upon each one's understanding the services the other is trying to perform. For this reason, a chapter has been included which defines, in general terms, some of the activities of co-ordinators, counselors, and advisers in agencies servicing the vocationally handicapped.

Agencies Servicing the Vocationally Handicapped

Vocational rehabilitation has been subsidized by federal funds since the passage of the first Rehabilitation Act in June, 1920. Until its amendment in 1943, the activities of the Vocational Rehabilitation Service were conducted in the states by the various State Boards of Vocational Education. Through the years this money, together with state and local funds, has been wisely spent.

Civilian rehabilitation is a multi-phased activity available to every physically handicapped person in the United States. Such individuals need only find the rehabilitation worker in the community and, if the handicapped person shows vocational potentialities, the trained case worker can be of great assistance. The service, which is free to the individual, includes five activities: guidance, restoration, training, placement, and follow-up. These are briefly described in the paragraphs which follow.

Guidance

Rehabilitation co-ordinators are frequently selected from among shop teachers or craftsmen who have had sufficiently diversified educational and vocational experience to enable them to analyze occupational information and the factual data of the case at hand. Usually these workers are given careful on-the-job training in techniques of getting case histories, conducting interviews, disseminating information, contacting employers, evaluating training, and co-operating with other agencies.

After taking a careful case history, the rehabilitation co-ordinator is in a better position to suggest possible types of training for the physically handicapped person. Occasionally, the local physician is contacted to make certain that the physical condition of the prospective rehabilitant is such that a training program should be launched. The rehabilitation co-ordinator points out avenues through which the handicapped may succeed. Selection of the goal and training preparatory to entering an occupation are the responsibility of the rehabilitant.

Restoration

Physical restoration may involve several types of treatment. An artificial appliance may be required, or medical attention may be needed; this service will be provided when the need has been determined. The co-ordinators work through local medical authorities, since co-ordinators usually are not skilled practitioners themselves. Rehabilitation workers strive to restore the individual to a condition as near normal as possible, so that acceptance of the applicant for placement may be assured.

Many rehabilitants are guided into occupations in which they can become self-employed. Shoe-, watch-, appliance-, and typewriter-repair shops are typical of the sort of arrangement that holds many possibilities for the physically handicapped. Even in these lines, however, restoration is important if the rehabilitant is to contact the general public. Money spent for plastic surgery can pay dividends to the public in this program of restoration.

Training

All training given rehabilitants is directed toward vocational adjustment and placement. Whenever the facilities of public vocational schools are used, guidance and training are closely co-ordinated. College courses are available to those who have demonstrated reasonable proficiency and show promise that they can and will succeed. Private schools that have demonstrated a sincere desire to help the handicapped also assist in preparing the handicapped to enter employment.

Most vocational and trade schools operated from public funds are visited regularly by a rehabilitation co-ordinator who serves the area in which the school is located. Not infrequently, the co-ordinator's headquarters are in the school building.

Complete rehabilitation service is available to plant workers who have been injured in industrial accidents. Of course, the Vocational Rehabilitation Service does not contemplate paying subsistence or maintenance for an individual prior to placement. Limited maintenance funds are available but, in the case of an industrial accident, the worker's own disability compensation, plus the other rehabilitation facilities present a unique plan of preparing a disabled worker to assume another occupation in making a job adjustment.

Placement

For more than twenty-five years, the Rehabilitation Service has carried on its own placement activity. Wherever feasible it has co-operated in utilizing the placement facilities of the State Employment Service.[1] Rehabilitation co-ordinators also maintain contact with industry. In the years since 1920 these men and women have achieved extraordinary success in job placement for the physically handicapped. No small part of their activity involves assisting rehabilitants to set up shops and work places of their own. The wisdom of this plan has manifested itself in the present drive for additional small business establishments. Flexibility of working hours and conveniently arranged work places

[1] For a sample of the kind of placement work possible with the physically handicapped see: H. A. Dreher, "Rating for the Handicapped," *Employment Security Review,* October, 1942, pages 15-16.

suited to the individual's needs make self-owned small shops for handicapped persons highly desirable.

Follow-up

The old saying, "The proof of the pudding . . ." might be paraphrased "The proof of the pudding is in the placement." Co-ordinators, working on this premise, follow-up rehabilitants who have entered employment. Everything within reason is done to make possible continuous, uninterrupted service to the employer by the rehabilitant.

Rehabilitants who meet the challenge know that upon the quality and continuity of the service they render an employer depends the future placement of others who need and want work. Fortunately for all concerned, records prove that physically handicapped workers, properly trained and well-placed, furnish continuous, better service than do those without handicaps.

Plant counselors should know the rehabilitation co-ordinator well. If no in-plant assistance is needed, perhaps some plant employee has a crippled son or daughter needing the kind of pre-vocational counseling that the skilled rehabilitation co-ordinator can supply.

The Local Employment Office

Although placement of the physically handicapped is not a new problem to local employment offices, the increased numbers of handicapped individuals resulting from combat injuries in World War II have accelerated the demand for improved services from the various placement departments of the Public Employment Service.[2] A program of selective placement for the physically handicapped was established in many local employment offices just prior to the abolition of the War Manpower Commission and the subsequent return of the Employment Service to the states.

[2] Charles Farmer, "The Task of the United States Employment Service in the Post-War Adjustment Period," *Personnel Administration*, January, 1945, pages 1-5.

It is possible that improved handling of the physically handicapped will result from their program.   Some private employment
agencies have accepted the challenge offered by the placement of
individuals who have physical handicaps.   The ability to perform
given tasks with speed and accuracy is a large factor in determining the acceptability of applicants by these agencies.

From contact with the Public Employment Service or private
employment agencies, the handicapped person usually obtains
pertinent information helpful in making the necessary adjustments
to his future work.   The experiences of an employment office
interview are sometimes unpleasant, but when the individual is
aware of the adjustments he must make, and determines to make
them, his job placement is closer to realization.

Associations for the Disabled

The National Rehabilitation Association, whose members are
laymen in the field of rehabilitation, has carried on a campaign
to encourage the physically handicapped.   The law occasionally
circumscribes a public agency to such an extent that deserving
individuals cannot be served adequately.   In such a case, the
association fills in the gaps and the program moves forward without interruption.

Not all legislation beneficial to the handicapped has developed
directly from legislative action.   Much of the spade-work has
been done by interested members of lay associations.   Frequently, whole communities have been aroused to the need for
co-operative effort in providing facilities that will help handicapped individuals become vocationally self-sufficient.

Some state associations affiliated with the National Association
for the Disabled have taken over the work involved in assisting
the handicapped with occupational adjustment problems.   Local
associations for the disabled have been helping needy handicapped
in many communities for years.   Financing local chapters has
not been a difficult task and funds gathered have been used to

purchase glasses, hearing aids, and artificial appliances for deserving cases. Others in need of small shop facilities have been set up in business by the association or its members.

Local chapters frequently get behind a sale of Easter seals and take a percentage of the proceeds from the International Society for Crippled Children. Usually, 100 seals about the size of a postage stamp are distributed with the idea of the recipient mailing one or more dollars to the association. The seals are used to brighten envelopes during the Easter season. These funds, together with those raised through membership fees, donations, and occasional participation in community chest funds, supply local chapters with the money needed to carry on their work.

Contact with any state or local chapter will bring information as to the specific cases aided through these associations. For example, the association's funds may offer the only chance a needy boy or girl has of obtaining glasses. Costs of transportation to and from clinics and hospitals, and for the fitting of artificial appliances, have been paid from the treasury of such associations. Money also has been provided for the essentials of maintenance while a handicapped person took a training course which would make him self-supporting. Money has helped provide essential pieces of equipment for the opening of a small business by a handicapped trainee. These are but a few of the helps provided by the branches or chapters of the National Association for the Disabled.

The Junior Chamber of Commerce, the Elks Club, the American Red Cross, the Veterans Administration, the County Veteran's Service Officer, and others interested in the problems of the handicapped frequently pool their efforts in a local chapter for the disabled. Usually each organization has its field of activity pretty well circumscribed, but an association for the disabled can function as a clearinghouse for all these agencies. Funds of independent organizations may or may not be used for certain specific types of assistance such as the purchase of glasses, hearing aids, wheelchairs, and the like, since limitations such as *age* and *need* are placed on Federal Civilian Rehabilitation funds. Through a clearinghouse arrangement, duplication of effort and wasting of funds are largely eliminated.

An association makes it possible for persons reporting cases to be assured that all agencies that should contact the case will be called upon, yet only one agency will furnish needed service, and a central file is kept which records all work done for the rehabilitant.

Counseling Handicapped Veterans

The problem of counseling veterans is an interesting one because of the numerous groups and agencies involved. Attached to many local employment offices are men who are responsible for seeing that counseling and placement opportunities are available to veterans. Finding the minimum requirements of each job and matching the physical capacities of the individual with the job requirements put new responsibilities upon those placing handicapped veterans. Seldom in our industrial history have we been so aware of the necessity for adequate placement of the handicapped as in the period following World War II.[3] The County Veteran's Service Officer is prepared to help veterans needing his advice. The various veterans organizations have committees and representatives designated to handle situations in which veterans need advice and counsel. The Veterans Administration has offices throughout the country for assisting handicapped veterans with information and guidance. Banks, real estate offices, large corporations, city governments, and many other organizations have individuals who counsel with veterans on a variety of matters.[4]

---

[3] This reference shows the readiness with which the problem has been attacked. David C. Post, "The Veterans' Problem—A Challenge and an Opportunity," *Personnel,* November, 1944, pages 126-130. New York: American Management Association.

[4] The community approach to the counseling of veterans has been helpful in coordinating the activities of the agencies rendering specific services. To get some conception of the varied nature of agencies concerned with the problems of adult counseling see: Helen H. Ringe, and others, "Counseling—Its Importance in the Transition from War to Peace," *Proceedings of the Thirty-Second Annual Convention of the International Association of Public Employment Services,* Milwaukee, 1944, pages 18-20.

Colleges and trade schools also have advisers to handle their special problems.

Of importance to the plant counselor is the fact that in nearly every instance, regardless of the problem to be met by an individual, there is some agency or some person who has been delegated to minister to that need. In cases where management desires to aid its own personnel and has set aside the funds to meet their needs, prompt relief can be given the physically handicapped employees. If funds are not available within the plant, the counselor will find a sizable group of people outside the plant who directly or indirectly have a responsibility for the training, welfare, and placement of the physically handicapped.[5]

Questions

1. Determine what rehabilitation services are available in your community. What changes in their organizational structure have taken place since the National Rehabilitation Act was revised in 1943.
2. Explain what is meant by the statement, "Civilian rehabilitation is a multi-phased activity."
3. Explain briefly the term *restoration* as applied to rehabilitation work.
4. Describe the background of an individual qualified for the position of rehabilitation co-ordinator.
5. How do physically handicapped workers compare with non-handicapped workers in regard to continuous, uninterrupted service to an employer?
6. List some services rendered by associations for the disabled.
7. Conduct a private survey to discover whether there is a public agency in your locality that can and will furnish glasses for a needy individual of employable age.
8. State the advantages of a clearinghouse for agencies attempting to meet the needs of the physically handicapped.
9. List several reasons why the plant counselor should know the co-ordinator, counselor, or adviser of agencies servicing the physically handicapped.

[5] Maj. Gen. Graves B. Erskine, "It's Good Business to Hire the Handicapped," *Domestic Commerce,* March, 1947, pages 21-25. Washington: Superintendent of Documents, Government Printing Office.

Bibliography

Bridges, Clark D., *Job Placement of the Physically Handicapped*. New York: McGraw-Hill Book Company, Inc., 1946.

Rogers, Carl R., and Wallen, John L., *Counseling with Returned Servicemen*. New York: McGraw-Hill Book Company, Inc., 1946.

Sullivan, O. M., and Snortum, K. O., *Disabled Persons, Their Education and Rehabilitation*. New York: Century Company, 1926.

Employment for the Handicapped. New York: The Russell Sage Foundation, 1927.

Counseling the Handicapped. New York: National Tuberculosis Association, 1940.

Publications of the United States Office of Education

Available from the Superintendent of Documents, Government Printing Office, Washington (25) D. C.

Manual for Case Workers, Vocational Rehabilitation, Vocational Education Bulletin No. 175, Rehabilitation Series No. 23, 1934.

Vocational Rehabilitation of the Physically Handicapped, Vocational Education Bulletin No. 190, Vocational Rehabilitation Series No. 25, 1936.

Workmen's Compensation Laws in Relation to Employment of the Physically Handicapped, Miscellaneous Bulletin 2152, Revised, 1941.

BECAUSE the number of handicapped persons is larger today than ever before, there is a growing need for counselors to study the question—How many physically handicapped workers should our plants employ?   This problem is a challenge to counselors because management needs an answer to it and other social problems that have an economic background.   Without applying any mathematical formula to the problem, the counselor might arrive at a reasonable plan through the following processes.

How Many Physically Handicapped?

Let us start with the assumption that the plant takes care of workers injured while on the job; this is fundamental.   It has been explained on page 49 that through workmen's compensation an employee can maintain himself and his family if retraining is necessary.   Through facilities of the State Rehabilitation program, the cost of the necessary training can be obtained.   With these as starters, the counselor (assisted by the Public Employment Service if he desires help) should be able to analyze plant operations to the point of determining what job best fits an injured worker.   This determination cannot be made without first knowing the worker's educational background, his aptitudes, visual and auditory acuity, past training, interests, and hobbies.   An appraisal from an attending physician as to the fitness of the individual for specific jobs should be obtained for placement purposes. Physical capacities forms available from the Public Employment Service are helpful in recording all pertinent factors.   For a sample of this form see page 58.

Through matching the capacities of the individual and the known demands of the job (see page 59) every plant could make full use of *all its own* injured workers.   Frequently, the procedure will result in increased production.   Many times a post-injury inventory is the first attempt on the part of the management to match the worker with the demands of a specific job.   When counseling has been well done, when physical capacities and physical demands are carefully matched, improved production is often the result.

Absorbing one's own industrial casualties is not sufficient, however; there are greater social obligations as well.   It is economically sound to have these people on a payroll rather than unemployed; the latter add to the taxes levied against a plant.   It is the opinion of the authors that the proportion of handicapped employees in every plant should be in direct ratio with the number of handicapped in the state where the plant is located.   The figure will probably vary between 5 per cent and 25 per cent depending on local conditions; an estimate of 15 handicaps per hundred workers is a fair anticipated average.   Surveys of the entire community should reveal the total number of handicapped persons in the area, whereas a single plant survey will not.

There are among the employees of many plants, workers who served in the armed forces.   Some of these individuals are seriously handicapped through the loss of limbs or eyesight, while others require a special diet, a special soap, or harmonious surroundings.   The counselor should be alert to the needs of these former servicemen.   The counselor should assist management through the making of factual studies of the production records, absences, complaints, suggestions, accident rates, quit rates, and similar items of importance in the employment of handicapped workers.

Analyzing an Industry for Selective Jobs

An employer desiring to hire physically handicapped persons in the community should seek the assistance of the Public Em-

Form ES-150
(Rev. 2-45)

Budget Bureau No. 11-R048.1
Approval Expires February 28, 1946

WAR MANPOWER COMMISSION

PHYSICAL CAPACITIES FORM

Name ___A. J. Allen___ Sex __M__ Age __28__ Height __68__ Weight __130__

PHYSICAL ACTIVITIES		WORKING CONDITIONS	
1 Walking	16 Throwing	51 Inside	✓ 66 Mechanical Hazards
2 Jumping	17 Pushing	52 Outside	✓ 67 Moving Objects
3 Running	18 Pulling	53 Hot	68 Cramped Quarters
4 Balancing	19 Handling	✓ 54 Cold	O 69 High Places
5 Climbing	20 Fingering	O 55 Sudden Temp. Changes	70 Exposure to Burns
6 Crawling	21 Feeling	56 Humid	71 Electrical Hazards
7 Standing	22 Talking	57 Dry	72 Explosives
8 Turning	23 Hearing	58 Wet	73 Radiant Energy
9 Stooping	24 Seeing	59 Dusty	74 Toxic Conditions
10 Crouching	✓ 25 Color Vision	60 Dirty	75 Working With Others
11 Kneeling	O 26 Depth Preception	61 Odors	76 Working Around Others
12 Sitting	27 Working Speed	62 Noisy	77 Working Alone
13 Reaching	28	63 Adequate Lighting	78
14 Lifting	29	64 Adequate Ventilation	79
✓ 15 Carrying	30	65 Vibration	80

Blank Space = Full Capacity: ✓ = Partial Capacity: O = No Capacity

May work_____ hours per day_____ days per week.   (If TB, cardiac or other disability
requiring limited working hours.)

May lift or carry up to_____ pounds.

Details of limitations for specific physical activities ___Should not be required to___
___look at close work for long period.___

_____

_____

Details of limitations for specific working conditions ___Must avoid prolonged___
___exposure to temperatures below 30°F. Should not work to left of mechanical___
___hazards or moving objects.___

_____

_____

_____

Date ___October 1, 1944___   Physician ___A. D. James, M. D.___

7-8495-44

A CAREFUL INVENTORY OF THE PHYSICAL CAPACITIES OF HANDICAPPED WORKERS RESULTS
IN IMPROVED JOB PLACEMENT.

Form ES-130
(3-44)

WAR MANPOWER COMMISSION
BUREAU OF MANPOWER UTILIZATION

Budget Bureau No. 11-R088.2.
Approval expires February 28, 1945.

PHYSICAL DEMANDS FORM

Job title ....Stonecutter..   Occupational code ..4-68.200....

Dictionary title ....STONECUTTER HAND II..

Firm name and address ....John Ramond Company, Chicago, Illinois................

Industry ....Stonework..   Industrial code ....3281........

Branch ..Cut Stone & Stone Products........   Department ....Cutting........

Company officer ....George Olson........   Analyst ..Robert Benson........   Date ..8-10-44....

PHYSICAL ACTIVITIES		WORKING CONDITIONS	
...X. 1. Walking.	..O..16. Throwing.	..X..51. Inside.	..X..66. Mechanical hazards.
..O. 2. Jumping.	..X..17. Pushing.	..X..52. Outside.	..X..67. Moving objects.
..O. 3. Running.	..X..18. Pulling.	..O..53. Hot.	..O..68. Cramped quarters.
..O. 4. Balancing.	..X..19. Handling.	..O..54. Cold.	..O..69. High places.
..O. 5. Climbing.	..X..20. Fingering.	..O..55. Sudden temp. changes.	..O..70. Exposure to burns.
..O. 6. Crawling.	..O..21. Feeling.	..O..56. Humid.	..O..71. Electrical hazards.
..X. 7. Standing.	..O..22. Talking.	..O..57. Dry.	..O..72. Explosives.
..X. 8. Turning.	..X..23. Hearing.	..O..58. Wet.	..O..73. Radiant energy.
..X. 9. Stooping.	..X..24. Seeing.	..X..59. Dusty.	..O..74. Toxic conditions.
..O.10. Crouching.	..O..25. Color vision.	..X..60. Dirty.	..X..75. Working with others.
..O.11. Kneeling.	..O..26. Depth perception.	..O..61. Odors.	..O..76. Working around others.
..O.12. Sitting.	..O..27. Working speed.	..X..62. Noisy.	..O..77. Working alone.
..X.13. Reaching.	......28.	..X..63. Adequate lighting.	......78.
..X.14. Lifting.	......29.	..X..64. Adequate ventilation.	......79.
..X.15. Carrying.	......30.	..X..65. Vibration.	......80.

16—30300-1   U. S. GOVERNMENT PRINTING OFFICE

Details of physical activities: Stands, stoops, walks, and turns to perform the following operations: Using both hands, arms, and fingers, reaches for, grasps, lifts and carries stones and slabs of marble weighing up to 75 pounds, and pushes and pulls on them to position them for cutting (1 hour). Uses both hands and arms to handle heavy hammers, mallets, pitching tool, pneumatic drills, T wrenches, emery wheel and various types of chisels to cut and polish stones and slabs (6 hours). Fingers folding rule, calipers, straightedge, and squares to measure stones for dimensions (1 hour). Pushes hand truck to transport material weighing up to 300 pounds and pulls on chainfall to operate overhead crane. Reads blueprints and observes stone or slabs for best cutting position and surface.

Details of working conditions: Works with others inside (3 hours) and outside (5 hours). Exposed to loud noises from pneumatic drill and constant hammering, dust and dirt from cutting and polishing operations, and vibration to body from operating drills.

Details of hazards: Possibility of bruises or cuts from chips or blocks of stone, of respiratory disorders from inorganic dust, and of injury from heavy stones falling on feet or hands.

THE PHYSICAL DEMANDS FORM AIDS IN MATCHING THE CAPACITIES OF AN INDIVIDUAL WITH THE PHYSICAL ACTIVITY REQUIREMENTS OF A SPECIFIC JOB.

ployment Service.[1]   The Employment Service has the necessary forms which list the physical demands of each job; job analysis will then reveal the physical qualities necessary to perform the tasks.

Samples of the Physical Capacities Appraisal and the Physical Demands forms are shown on pages 58 and 59.   When a complete job analysis of a plant has been made, management is in an excellent position to estimate the number of physically handicapped workers that could be used advantageously.

Some employers will want to use a committee in determining the jobs which the handicapped might perform.   In this situation, an employer might ask a representative of the Public Employment Service and the State Rehabilitation Service to meet with the personnel director or the counselor to prepare a plan that will permit the plant to absorb workers into certain jobs which are determined to be readily adaptable to physically handicapped individuals.   This committee would work out, co-operatively, such details as the employer deemed to be within the scope of the committee.   Consideration might also be given to selecting an employee representative who is on the same job level as the plant's union representative, but who speaks for the employees at large, rather than for the union, specifically.

The committee would formulate all plans for making the analysis, and would meet from time to time to examine the data and to recommend changes which would improve the analysis. The committee's actions could form the basis for news stories when the management is ready to announce its policy on employment of the physically handicapped.   Finally, the committee would be in a position to make recommendations in the report submitted upon completion of the study.   The impartiality of the survey and the progressive attitude of the employer in planning to absorb his share of the physically handicapped in the com-

---

[1] For a complete treatise on the techniques of utilizing handicapped workers see: *Selective Placement for the Handicapped, Revised,* Bureau of Placement, Department of Labor.   Washington: Superintendent of Documents, Government Printing Office.

munity should be given widespread newspaper publicity. The employment of the less fortunate workers in the community is good for top newspaper billing any time and the employer who helps them deserves much credit and commendation.

Advantages in Employing Handicapped Workers

A growing number of employers are making an effort to employ handicapped workers; the tight wartime labor market forced other employers to take this step. Among the latter can be counted the supporters of the movement today. Stability of the work force was important during the war, and handicapped workers proved themselves to be more steady than non-handicapped workers. Lower turnover rates, greater loyalty, more drive, and an eagerness to work are the results that have been obtained where the matching of worker and job has been given proper consideration. Here is an example that occurred in the early days of rehabilitation. A structural steel plant analyzed its operations for jobs for the handicapped. Studies showed that one-armed men could paint structural pieces if these were laid on the ground before being shipped to an erection point. One-armed men were put to work painting the steel. Their production was equal to or above that of two-armed painters; they stayed with the work longer, and they were considered to be a decided asset by their employer. There are hundreds of other more recent examples that are equally convincing. This example was cited because there are few who would believe that one-armed painters could succeed in any field.

There seems to be evidence which proves that properly placed physically handicapped persons can compete with non-handicapped workers on many jobs.[2] Disabled persons usually put forth more effort to hold their jobs; they are less likely to leave a job; they lose less time and seem less accident prone than other workers.

[2] *Employment Efficiency of Physically Impaired Workers,* Federal Security Agency, U. S. Office of Education, Vocational Rehabilitation Division. Washington: Superintendent of Documents, Government Printing Office, May, 1943.

Hundreds of handicapped workers are being trained annually by the Rehabilitation Service. These men and women are entering small businesses of their own in great numbers because they find it difficult to get on an employer's payroll. If these people succeed in private business they must be average, or above-average, in skill and ability. This being the case, they should be a good risk on industry's payroll. Each of these successful business men becomes a potential competitor of a plant or an industry. Such growth is good from the consumer's point of view, but what about it from the producer's point of view?

Counselors can render a great service to employers and the whole rehabilitation movement by familiarizing themselves with the Compensation Laws covering the employment of physically handicapped persons. Frequently, the Rehabilitation Co-ordinator serving the area in which the plant is located can be of assistance in securing copies of laws, rules, and regulations.

A Philosophy for Counselors Towards the Handicapped

The success of any program for hiring the physically handicapped will depend almost entirely upon proper selection and placement. They should be assigned to jobs where they can compete (with reasonable opportunity for success) with non-handicapped workers. The handicapped worker needs to be challenged; but he should not be overwhelmed before he gets under-way.

Much more counseling and training is available to physically handicapped persons than is available to the non-handicapped. Under certain conditions it is possible for an employer to be compensated for training handicapped workers to be used in his own establishment. Abuses have occurred recently in "On-the-Job" training of veterans; the matter of compensating an employer for training his own workers therefore must be evaluated more carefully. There is ample opportunity for the training of handicapped workers in some vocational or trade school within the state.

Long-term training is available to individuals who have demonstrated a capacity to profit by higher education, and college-trained rehabilitants are being turned out each year. Rehabilitants with four years of higher education should come to the employer reasonably well-selected and adequately prepared for the job.[3]

It is important that not too much sentiment enter into dealings with the handicapped. They, least of all, want charity; they want, most of all, an opportunity. Given an opportunity, most handicapped workers will come through in a manner that will bring an employer's attitude and philosophy towards handicaps to new heights of acceptance. In getting started, the counselor may obtain the assistance of the Public Employment Service and the Rehabilitation Service; both have many skilled workers who may be called upon.

Counselors must study the field of employment for the physically handicapped. There are laws, insurance regulations, safety factors, economic conditions and other items to be considered when approaching the subject from an objective point of view. It is suggested that the counselor get the facts well in hand before launching upon any management-selling campaign. Employers with the most liberal point of view toward hiring of the handicapped are those that established carefully thought-out programs for their integration in the work force. To start slowly and build soundly is of greatest importance to the counselor interested in the wise use of the physically handicapped.

Placing the Handicapped to Advantage

Placing the handicapped worker to advantage means placing him in a job that is within his physical powers of performance; in addition, there should be some mental challenge or competitive features which test his thinking. The *physical demands analysis,* a phase of job analysis, points the way to the physical requirements of a specific job. The *physical capacities appraisal* gives the probable capacity of the individual to perform certain move-

[3] For a discussion of the techniques involved in selling the employer see: *Selective Placement for the Handicapped,* War Manpower Commission, United States Employment Service, pages 24-30. Washington: Superintendent of Documents, Government Printing Office, December, 1943.

ments under given conditions. The matching of the physical capacities with the physical requirements of the job forms the basis of placing the handicapped to advantage.[4] In modern plants, work simplification and improved job techniques have helped to eliminate the squinting, squatting, stretching, or straining. This is an advantage for the handicapped worker. Where management has not brought job techniques up-to-date, the needed improvements, if made, should form a good starting point preliminary to the employment of handicapped workers.

Following the simplification of various operations, the physical demands analysis should be completed. These two steps are basic to the placement procedure. Applicants could be interviewed while the first two steps were being taken. The physical capacities of workers could thus be catalogued for future comparison and matching with job specifications.

Physical and mental capacity will be the major limitations which govern the placement of those seeking employment. It should be possible to work out training programs that will prepare those not already experienced for entrance into the specific jobs selected for them. Matching should be done carefully, and it is suggested that outside help be secured in initiating this program. Here again, the Rehabilitation Service, the Public Employment Service,[5] the State Commission for the Blind, or some other specialized branch of the state's Welfare Department may render valuable service in getting the placement program underway. The counselor will find it advantageous to keep in touch with these and other public agencies interested in the welfare of individuals who make up the labor force of the community. Programs of a public nature are subject to constant change. The alert counselor will want to keep informed of progress being made in the community.

[4] *National Physical Demands Information,* Series: Number I, *Apprenticeable Occupations,* November, 1944, 112 pages. Available in most Public Employment Offices.

[5] Raymond C. Atkinson, Louise C. Odencrange, and Ben Deming, *Public Employment Service in the United States,* pages 394-403. Chicago: Public Administration Service, 1938.

Results of a Good Program

Correct placement of the handicapped worker, matching of the man and the job, is a most important step, but the personnel job does not end here.   Follow-up action should be taken to determine progress of the worker from time to time.   Possibly, some follow-up may be made during the first few days.   Then, at increasingly wider intervals, additional follow-up measures should be taken to determine the degree to which the worker has become adjusted to his job.   Only through follow-up can the results of a good placement job be ascertained.   Results of a good program are not to be discussed here in terms of specific plants, although reference could be made to the good work of the Western Electric Company and others.   The real outcomes are best measured in terms of industry's efforts to absorb an ever-increasing number of handicapped workers.   There are certain social values which accrue to the employer and the community as a result of the self-respect afforded those individuals who have been given an opportunity to become breadwinners rather than the objects of charity. Fruitage comes, too, when the employer realizes that the handicapped men and women whom he has employed have not taken advantage of him but are pulling their share of the load.   The transformation of a social responsibility to a social and economic asset is a worthy outcome.

The employment of handicapped persons provides the answer to many of the inner drives and urges felt by all humans.   The achievement of these motives and ambitions often defies measurement, but we can see the appreciation mirrored in the faces of those whom we have helped to help themselves.   The counselor will want to study carefully the placement of the physically handicapped and make sound appraisals before making specific recommendations as to the numbers of individuals that management should place on its payrolls.[6]   The advantageous use of handi-

---

[6] For a discussion of the handicapped in the Union contract concerning such matters as wages, conditions of employment, and seniority, consult Leonard J. Smith, *Collective Bargaining*, pages 91, 157-158, 194-195. New York: Prentice-Hall, Inc., 1946.

capped workers in optimum numbers should be the goal of the counselor. The correct number can be determined only after careful, objective research and study.

Questions

1. Explain the terms *Physical Capacities Appraisal* and *Physical Demands Analysis*.
2. What percentage of employees should be selected from among the physically handicapped?
3. Explain what factors will help to insure success in an accelerated program of hiring physically handicapped workers.
4. Discuss some reasons why a single survey might not uncover all physically handicapped workers on a plant payroll.
5. State at least five items that could be used to prove the economic value of handicapped workers.
6. Describe the placement activity of the Rehabilitation Service in your State.
7. Explain the "clearinghouse" idea carried on by some associations for the disabled.
8. Describe the process of analyzing an industrial plant for the selective placement of handicapped workers.
9. Check the Workmen's Compensation Laws in your state to determine whether or not subsistence could be paid an injured worker while he is being retrained for a new job in the same plant.
10. Visit the Public Employment Office in your community to determine what facilities are available for placing physically handicapped individuals.

Bibliography

Dallas, Herbert A., "Problems of One-Arm Cases," *National Rehabilitation News*, April, 1943.

Dietz, J. W., "Experiment with Vocationally Handicapped Workers," *Personnel Journal*, February, 1932.

Kratz, J. A., "Rehabilitation and Placement of the Physically Disabled," *Employment Service News*, August, 1935.

Rose, Marc A., "A Blind Worker in Every Factory," *Reader's Digest*, Vol. 32, No. 189, January, 1938, pages 93-95.

THE complete readjustment and re-employment of veterans will be a challenge to industry and to the entire nation for some time to come. Each phase of economic adjustment following the war will present new problems to industrial establishments in their handling of veterans. Increased employment means the hiring of larger quotas of former servicemen and the problems attendant to such groups. For example, there will be the need for training programs to permit upgrading of workers, recreational facilities to keep young men from changing jobs frequently, and supervisors will need specific help in dealing with individuals whose backgrounds in travel, discipline, and previous work differ from those of non-veterans. Any reductions in personnel will carry a great responsibility to deal fairly with those men deserving better than average treatment. Fortunately, our present consideration can be focused upon the rehiring and the integrating of veterans into an era of expanding business opportunities. Government agencies have been given new responsibilities in the veteran program,[1] and certain industrial plants have done an outstanding job of fitting veterans into their day-to-day operations.

The United States Department of Labor
Veterans' Counseling Program of the U. S. Employment Service

In 1946, the United States Employment Service became a division within the United States Department of Labor, but the

---

[1] Veterans Administration, "Counseling Services of the Veterans Administration," *Manpower Review,* March, 1945, pages 10-11.

regional offices operate under the old title, USES, and retain the function of supervising the standards of performance in the State Employment Service offices. However, the reorganization and name-changing has not affected the USES's veterans' counseling program.

Since the counseling is federally subsidized, it has remained intact while many other activities of the United States Employment Service have reverted to state supervision. The services available to veterans merit the attention of counselors and others concerned with the welfare of the ex-serviceman. Regardless of the label on the door of your Public Employment Service, there is, without a doubt, a uniformly high quality, federally operated veterans' counseling program operating in that office.

Congress has enacted a series of laws in an attempt to secure for the veteran an effective counseling and job placement service. Title IV of Public Law 346—78th Congress, declares that the purpose of this legislation is "to provide an effective job counseling and employment placement service" for veterans.[2] The intent of the legislation is to furnish the maximum of opportunities for gainful employment. The Act provides further for the creation of a Veterans' Placement Service Board to assist and co-operate with the United States Employment Service. The Board consists of the Administrator of Veterans' Affairs as chairman, the Director of the Office of Selective Service Records, and either the Administrator of the Federal Security Agency, or whoever may have the responsibility for administering the U. S. Employment Service. The Board's primary function is to determine policies relating to the administration of the Veterans' Employment Service activities in the USES. Responsibility for carrying out the policies rests with the Board chairman and the Veterans' Employment Representatives in each state. The law provides that the chairman may delegate to an executive secretary the necessary authority to act as Chief of the Veterans' Employment Service.

---

[2] Copies of the Act are available from the Superintendent of Documents, Washington, D. C., Public Law 346, Chapter 268, 78th Congress, Second Session.

The Act requires that each of the Veterans' Employment Representatives be a veteran of World Wars I and II, a resident within the state, be separated from actual military service, be appointed according to Civil Service regulations, and that USES's appointment be approved by the Veterans' Placement Service Board. Each representative is administratively responsible to the Board through the Chief of the Veterans' Employment Service. In the execution of the Board's placement policies, each representative reports to the Employment Service head in his state.

The veterans' representative is also directed to co-operate with the federally subsidized counseling staff of the USES in order that the five major objectives of the Act may be achieved.

(1) He shall supervise the registration of veterans in local employment offices. It is his duty to see that suitable jobs are made available from those orders received from prospective employers.

(2) He will secure and furnish current information as to the kinds of available jobs in public work and in private industry.

(3) The representative will encourage the employment of veterans by employers.

(4) He will perform liaison functions between employers and veterans' organizations, keeping employers informed of likely candidates for such openings as occur.

(5) He is to assist wherever possible in improving working conditions for veterans. His responsibility includes looking out for the advancement or promotion of veterans to better positions.

The heads of the State Employment Service may designate a veteran already in their organization to assist the state representative of the Veterans' Employment Service in his duties.

All federal agencies have been instructed to furnish the Board with records, statistics, and other information that will facilitate veteran job placement.[3] It is hoped that this set-up will provide maximum employment opportunities for the veteran.

---

[3] For complete details see: Public Law 346, Title IV, Chapter 6, *Employment of Veterans,* Section 601. For further information about the Army and Navy readjustment programs, reference to the following articles is recommended: Lt. Comdr.

SUBJECT	AGENCY
1. Employment	1. Railroad Retirement Board
	2. State Merit System or Civil Service Commission
	3. War Shipping Administration
	4. Municipal Civil Service Commission
	5. County Agricultural Agent
	6. United States Civil Service Commission
2. Compensation	1. American Red Cross
	2. American Legion
	3. Disabled American Veterans
	4. Veterans of Foreign Wars
	5. American Veterans World War II
	6. United Spanish War Veterans
	7. R.V.A. (Regular Veterans Association)
	8. Military Order of the Purple Heart
	9. Army and Navy Units
	10. Jewish War Veterans
	11. Catholic War Veterans
	12. Veterans Administration
	13. Others
3. Family Service and Emergencies	1. United States Army Emergency Relief
	2. Navy Relief Society
	3. Red Cross
	4. All veterans organizations
4. Immigration	1. Bureau of Immigration and Naturalization, United States Department of Justice
5. Life Insurance	1. Veterans Administration
	2. County and State Service offices
6. Legal Advice	1. Local Re-employment Committees
	2. Local Bar Committees where available
7. Medical Service	1. Veterans Administration
	2. Local hospitals and clinics when available
	3. Red Cross
8. Mortuary Expense	1. Veterans Administration
9. Medals	1. All veterans organizations

At present, authority for the continuance of the Veterans' Employment Service rests with the Department of Labor which administers skeleton USES regional offices throughout the country. Local employment and placement offices operated by the states are wholly subsidized by federal funds. The quality of service rendered by state employment offices is maintained at a constant level by inspection from the regional offices.

A variety of organizations, Federal, State, County and private, chief among them the Veterans Administration, provides counseling facilities to assist the veteran with some of his other problems.

The Du Pont Veteran Employee Training Program

The Personnel Division of the Du Pont Company's Service Department division has prepared for plant foremen and supervisors a nine-hour program of six meetings designed to stimulate thinking on veteran readjustment problems.[4] Several foremen and supervisors assisted the personnel division in planning the training program. The first meeting of the series is informational, and is followed by five supervised conferences.

The program opens with a brief statement by the leader of the aims of the VET (Veteran Employee Training) Program, followed by a sound slide-film requiring 25 minutes running time. Part I of the film, "They'll Be Coming Home," presents the case of a returning employee, a veteran, who shows up at a plant that is not prepared for him. After some rough, inconsiderate treatment, the veteran begins to wonder about his sacrifices and his prospects for the future.

Part II shows the contrasted situation when the same plant is ready for the returning veteran. Definite techniques are being

---

John W. Corris, USNR, "Navy's Civil Readjustment Program," *Manpower Review*, March, 1945, pages 15-16. Major General Joe N. Dalton, USA, "Army Counseling Programs," *Manpower Review*, March, 1945, pages 12-13.

[4] The Du Pont Company produced an excellent manual, film strip, recording, and the necessary materials to do a real job of integrating returning veterans into their expanded operations. The initials *VET* were used to designate this Veteran Employee Training program developed by the Service Department, Du Pont Company, Wilmington, Del.

used to help him meet his problems and to make him feel at home. He is given an opportunity to "visit around," note changes, and to recognize developments that have taken place in his absence. The foremen contribute facts that will aid him in selecting the department where he desires to work.

After the film showing, the plant manager discusses the legal and moral responsibilities related to the re-employment of veterans. He gives the group an overview of the plant program for absorbing former service-connected employees.

To assist the Du Pont foremen and supervisors, some *tools*— data sheets—are furnished around which the five conference meetings are developed. They are:

1. *Supervisory Problem Sheet.* This furnishes clues to certain problems that will probably confront the foremen attempting to re-adjust veterans to production activities. The sheet, distributed at the first meeting, forms a springboard for the conference discussions that follow.

2. (a) *Facts to Consider—About the Veteran, Prior to Induction* raises seven questions:

1. What was his last job and rate?
2. Is he a temporary or permanent employee?
3. How much company service does he have?
4. What was his educational background?
5. What other plant jobs has he held?
6. What were his strong points? Weak points?
7. What other personal data should be considered?

(b) *Facts to Consider—War Experiences.* Physical disabilities and the rank or rating attained are points questioned here. Reference is made to a change in attitude, should this be recognized by the foreman. Six questions have been prepared for the foreman's consideration.

1. How long has he been in the service?
2. What special training did he receive?

3. How much combat experience has he had?
4. What physical disabilities have resulted from war experiences?
5. What rank or other special recognition has he attained?
6. Has his attitude changed toward the job; fellow workers; supervisors?

3. *About the Plant* presents facts which should be called to the attention of the returnee. Seven questions are included on the sheet.

1. What plant practices or customs have changed?
2. What rules or regulations have been changed?
3. What changes have been made in his job?
4. How does the product differ?
5. What changes have been made in the plant or departmental layout?
6. What personnel changes have been made?
7. What changes have been made in employee benefits or services?

4. *Setting the Stage,* a breakdown sheet, is next prepared by each supervisor attending the meetings. Armed with the data obtained for the *Facts to Consider* sheets, the foremen and supervisors then review each item in the light of their own veteran returnees. The group leader advises them to talk first with the fellow about to be displaced who assumed the veteran's job when the latter was inducted. In some instances, adjustments may have to be made to reopen the veteran's position. The foreman will list the key points he wishes to make when talking to the incumbent worker.

A second reminder on the breakdown sheet calls the attention of foreman and supervisors to the fact that they must talk with fellow workers of the returning veteran, either individually or in a group meeting. Anticipated questions from fellow workers might include: (1) Could we have a party in his honor? (2) What will happen to us—will we lose our jobs to returning veterans? (3) Is the veteran legally entitled to the job? (4) Should we double up and let him take it easy for a couple of weeks?

A third notation on the breakdown sheet is a reminder to select and prepare a job instructor who is acquainted with all facts on the returnee, and who will assist the veteran in "getting back on the beam" quickly and smoothly. The job instructor is usually a fellow employee of the veteran who has had previous instruction in training techniques. All three reminders facilitate the readjustment of the former employee.

5. *Off to the Right Start,* a second breakdown sheet, follows the conventional pattern of Steps and Key Points. Step one is "Greeting the Veteran," and space is provided to list those items which will make the greeting warm and friendly—a handshake, and perhaps some comment about personal affairs which may have changed during the absence of the employee. From this tip-off, the conversation swings to "Talking About the Job." To obtain the key points for the breakdown sheet, the foreman refers to his *Facts to Consider* list.

A third consideration, "Explaining Plant Changes," requires the foreman to use the *Facts* in order to identify changes that may have occurred; the result is a personalized analysis of the plant and the individual. Of course, it would be unnecessary to recite facts concerning changes which had occurred while the worker was still in the plant, and too impersonal to tell of changes that affect only workers in other departments.

Step four, "Getting Facts and Opinions" from fellow workers, may also play a vital part in the complete readjustment of the individual. When there is strong sentiment against the return of a specific individual, the foreman will have to make plans that provide for utilizing the individual elsewhere and revise the proposed schedule of reorientation. A fifth step, "Introducing the Veteran," and a sixth, "Showing Him Around," complete the items in the process of getting the returnee off to the right start on his post-war job. Each step is thought out in advance and every attempt is made to eliminate mistakes which might seriously hamper the quick, smooth readjustment of a deserving employee.

6. *Following His Progress,* another breakdown sheet, lists three steps in a sequence that is quite useful: (1) Information to be passed on during daily contacts; (2) Things to look for in daily contacts; (3) Problems to talk over with line organization members, medical personnel, and the counselor.

Two additional tools are also included in the VET plan: a detailed *Retraining Plan for the Specific Veteran,* and a *Physical Requirements Analysis of the Job.* The latter closely follows one used by the United States Employment Service, and fits well into the pattern of personnel practices.

In the second session, the *Facts to Consider* sheet and the pattern of the VET program is introduced. It is pointed out to the group that the *Facts* sheet forms the basis for all decisions to be made later in handling the readjustment problems of the veteran.

The third meeting provides practice in *Setting the Stage.* Each participant brings in a set of facts concerning a former employee. The members of the group demonstrate how these facts may be used in getting ready for the returnee. The demonstration includes talking with the worker about to be displaced, and with the individual who is to serve as instructor for the veteran.

Getting the veteran off to the right start is the theme of the fourth meeting. Each supervisor tells what he plans to cover with his employee, and all steps in the breakdown sheet explained on page 73 are followed closely. The fifth meeting covers specific techniques for giving the returnee the necessary job training. Special problems are discussed in this meeting and an opportunity for the exchange of ideas is provided.

The sixth and final meeting is devoted to *Following His Progress Closely.* Emphasis is placed upon supervisory problems that arise after reinduction and retraining. Stress is laid on getting the veteran into the normal routine of the plant at an early date.

The VET program is one of the best of its kind. It contains many elements of the pattern established during World War II by the Training Within Industry Service of the former War Manpower Commission, Federal Security Agency. The principles are, of course, observed in many of their non-veteran employee training programs, also. The program is recommended to plants interested in doing a real counseling job on the supervisory level. It should be pointed out that this program places tremendous responsibility upon the foreman for the gathering of factual data, making analyses, and contacting plant personnel. If production schedules are maintained during this period it is because the Du Pont plants have supervisors capable of a high level of performance not generally possible in chaotic times. Many of the human relations problems involved in the re-establishing of veterans on the job might well be handled jointly by the foreman and a counselor—the specialist in human relations problems.

The Veterans Administration

Counseling veterans for a return to industry seems to be the responsibility of several agencies and individuals. In a bulletin issued by the United States Government entitled *Your Rights and Benefits*,[5] the veteran is told to report to his Selective Service Board within five days of his discharge. Ex-service women are not required to report but they are advised to do so if they desire aid in securing re-employment. Now that the Selective Service Boards no longer function, veterans who have re-employment problems are advised to contact their county re-employment committeeman. The latter's name and address may be secured from the nearest local employment office. This bulletin serves as a counseling device, for it tells the veteran, among other things, to apply for his old job within 90 days after the date of discharge from the service. Those desiring re-employment by their former

---

[5] This pamphlet explaining veterans' rights and benefits under the G. I. Bill of Rights is available in most Public Employment Services and Veterans Administration Offices.

employer must meet the following qualifications: (1) the former position must have been other than temporary; (2) military service completed must have been satisfactory; (3) the individual must be qualified to perform the duties required.

For new employment, the veteran is told that the State Employment Service is ready and willing to help. Civil Service preference and other assistance is available to those desiring to get into governmental service. *Your Rights and Benefits*, prepared for veterans and their dependents, states in part:

> If you were a Federal Civil Service employee (other than temporary) when you entered the war, you should apply to the agency where last employed within 90 days of your discharge or to the Civil Service Commission in the event you experience difficulty in being reinstated. If you satisfy the requirements (see "Getting Your Old Job Back" above), you are entitled to your former position or one "of like seniority, status, and pay."
>
> If you didn't have a Civil Service job before, but want to get one after you are discharged, you will get special consideration and preference in Civil Service examinations. This preference also applies to wives or widows of veterans under certain circumstances.
>
> All wartime veterans discharged under honorable conditions are entitled to preference in U. S. Civil Service examinations. The entitlement to 5 or 10 points will be determined by the Civil Service Commission upon application to the Commission.
>
> Other privileges for veterans are:
>
> (1) Examination for positions of guard, elevator operator, messenger, and custodian will be restricted to veterans as long as veteran applicants are available.
>
> (2) Time spent in military service will be credited toward experience required for a position of the kind you left.
>
> (3) Age, height, and weight requirements are waived for veterans in most instances. Other physical requirements *may* be waived.
>
> (4) Veterans are exempted from provisions of law prohibiting government employment to more than two members of a family.

(5) If an appointing officer passes over a veteran and selects a non-veteran, he must submit his reasons in writing to the Civil Service Commission.

(6) In personnel reductions in any Federal agency, preference in retention will be given to veterans.

There are approximately 4,500 local Civil Service Secretaries located in all first- and second-class post offices, who will advise you concerning government employment, or such information may be secured from your Re-employment Committeeman or the U. S. Employment Service, who will put you in touch with a representative of the Civil Service Commission.

The benefits of apprenticeship are briefly explained, and the individual is again directed to the State Employment Service for assistance.

In the "Vocational Training" section of the bulletin reference is made to the Rehabilitation Service and the Veterans Administration.   Other literature of the Veterans Administration seems to tie their counseling service closely to the rehabilitation of the handicapped.   Veterans without special problems may find their way into industry through the routine channels of the Re-employment Committeeman, the Employment Service office, the local Veterans' Employment representative, or by direct application to a private employer.

The Handicapped Veteran

In the matter of the handicapped veteran, the outlook seems quite different.   The Veterans Administration had this to say about counseling:

In developing the counseling procedures it was necessary to give especial consideration to the provisions of the law which emphasize the employability and vocational adjustment aspects of the Veterans Administration program.   Accordingly, a *Manual of Advisement and Guidance* (U. S. Government Printing Office, Washington, 1945) was prepared to provide a procedure which would place emphasis upon the application of the basic principles of vocational counseling, but at the same time, insure that these principles would be supplemented by and co-ordinated with other phases of counseling according to the needs in the individual case. The procedures outlined in the Manual require that each veteran will be counseled as a person regarded as a complete entity with reference to his needs. These needs may call for the application of any of the specialized counseling techniques such as those of personal adjustment counseling at any stage during the counseling process. The procedures imply a thoroughness in counseling which enlists the aid of social case-work agencies in solving difficult family and financial problems and psychiatric care in the treatment of major personal-social-emotional problems. Thus the counseling of veterans varies in complexity according to the individual case and cannot be done adequately by strict adherence to time limits for the handling of each case or by ignoring in pertinent instances the assistance of the social worker or the psychiatrist or by failure to make follow-up studies in complex cases.

The counseling procedures that have been formulated are based on the principle that the veteran should be assisted in gaining insight into his vocational, educational and related problems in order to prepare himself to make his own decisions. The counselor assists the veteran in making an objective appraisal of his potentialities and limitations, and discusses occupational and educational goals, education and training facilities, personality traits, family conditions and other relevant matters with the veteran so that the veteran is able to appreciate and understand the significance of such factors in selecting a particular course of training or education. Every effort is made to stimulate the veteran to develop an attitude of self-help in order that he may take the responsibility for deciding his own course of action.[6]

Educational guidance and personal adjustment counseling are also available under the Veterans Administration plan. Those interested in the activities of a counselor in a University Guidance

[6] Ira D. Scott and Clyde J. Lindley, "The Advisement and Guidance Program of the Veterans Administration," *The American Psychologist*, June, 1946, pages 190-200.

Center for Veterans should read Robert H. Mathewson's account.[7] These services are an entirely different story and are not closely related to the problems of counseling veterans for entrance into industrial pursuits.

Questions

1. Prepare an organization chart showing the relationship of the United States Department of Labor, the United States Employment Service, the State Employment Service and your local Public Employment Office.

2. How has the return of the Employment Service to the states affected the Veterans' Counseling Service?

3. What agency provides funds for the operation of the Veterans Placement Service?

4. Name three agencies that might assist a veteran who is having trouble collecting unemployment compensation.

5. What is the nature of the Du Pont nine-hour program for supervisors?

6. Name two *tools* used by Du Pont foremen in the readjustment of veterans.

7. In the Du Pont program what is gained by talking to fellow workers of a returning veteran?

8. What is meant by "Explaining Plant Changes" to a veteran?

9. List the services rendered under the Vocational Advisement program of the United States Employment Service.

10. What is meant by placement counseling as applied to the veterans program of the Employment Service?

Bibliography

Counseling and Postwar Educational Opportunities, Volume VIII, May, 1944. Washington: American Counsel on Education Studies, Committee on Student Personnel Work.

"Counseling Service of the Veterans Administration," *Manpower Review,* March, 1945, Vol. 12, No. 3.

---

[7] Robert H. Mathewson, "The Vocational Appraiser in a University Veterans' Guidance Center," *Occupations,* October, 1945. New York: National Vocational Guidance Association.

Employers' Guide for Development of a Veterans Employment Program, Veterans Employment Service, United States Employment Service, U. S. Department of Labor.   Washington: Superintendent of Documents, Government Printing Office.

The American Legion Program for Veterans' Employment.   Washington, D. C.: National Employment Committee, The American Legion.

The Corpus Christi Plan for Veteran Placement.   The Chamber of Commerce, Corpus Christi, Texas.

Veteran Employee Training.   Wilmington, Del.: Personnel Division, Service Department, Du Pont Corporation.

WHEN dealing with special groups, care must be exercised to avoid typing or labeling counselees. Superficial observations and the readiness to apply mass formulae are shoals upon which a counseling program can founder quickly. In no other field of counseling is there a need for keener perception than in analyzing the problems and the facts presented by the members of special groups. Prejudices, wrong inferences, shallow interpretations, and other human weaknesses militate against complete satisfaction for the individuals that we think of as comprising the special groups. National characteristics, racial qualities, regional differences, and language difficulties can play tricks on the judgment of even the seasoned counselor.[1]

Using the Interview with Special Groups

Proper phraseology and timing of questions are important techniques that the counselor should learn to use adroitly. With special groups, leading questions frequently elicit the expected reply. However, the counselor should never expect a specific or predetermined reply to a stated question. Influencing the counselee through inflection or emphasis as to the kind of answer to be given happens all too frequently. It is perhaps the greatest single factor contributing to a counselor's failure to prove of full value to an employer. When a specific type of answer is implied in the question, the counselee is quick to sense what is desired in

---

[1] For an interesting discussion of the factors that affect complete understanding among individuals and groups see: William Albig, *Public Opinion,* pages 26-52. New York: McGraw-Hill Book Company, 1939.

an answer and usually says what he thinks should be said. Such information may bear little relationship to true facts. Erroneous decisions on the part of the counselor result from the use of data obtained in this manner.

In any situation where language difficulty or lack of understanding is encountered, questioning becomes an art upon which success or failure rests. Patience and persistence bring good returns if employed when interviewing clients whose background and environment differ widely from that of the counselor. Under all conditions, the counselor must be free of bias and prejudices for or against the counselee's background.

When assisting counselees in formulating their plan of action, counselors should remember that social custom, sentiment, and emotional factors often play a greater role in our lives than does logical reasoning or scientific planning.[2] Regardless of how right the scientific planning might be, many individuals would rather follow tradition than be right; in fact, they feel that by following tradition they are bound to be right. Standards of living vary greatly among groups as well as within a given group. The tendency on the part of individuals to be bound to their own group traditions should be taken into account when counseling members of various social and economic groups.

The manner in which people react to situations is governed by their desires, ambitions, fears, experiences, and drives. A personal philosophy of what is morally and socially right or wrong plays a great part in the lives of individuals.

Regardless of the qualities we attribute to groups, each counselee is an individual and the counselor must never lose sight of the fact.[3] The application of mass formulae proves to be a fallacy when applied to counseling procedure. The possible combina-

---

[2] For further discussion of the fundamental law of association see: R. L. Thomas and John H. Muchmore, "Getting Results in 'Problem' Interviews," *Personnel*, July, 1944, pages 31-37. New York: American Management Association.

[3] Individual differences in abilities and capacity to adjust must be considered when working with counselees. Percival M. Symonds, "How People Differ From One Another," *Personnel Journal*, February, 1945, pages 303-311.

tions that might go to make up these special groups is infinite. Certain characteristics of a few well-known groups with which the counselor is likely to come in contact are described below.

Older Workers

Much misinformation has been given out about older workers. The experiences of industry during World War II tended to disprove rather conclusively many of the patent statements concerning individuals who had passed the so-called period of prime physical output.   War industries' evidence seems to indicate that older workers frequently have a lower accident rate than the average for all industrial workers.   Taken as a group their absenteeism and tardiness rates are lower than the average.   The fact that older workers produced much vital war material by supplying shipyards, airplane factories, and munitions plants with their badly needed, scarce skills indicates that, prior to the war, there was misplaced prejudice against the employment of older workers.

However, when accidents do occur to those of advanced age, the severity is greater since older employees do not always have the reserve strength which permits them to "snap out of it" like youngsters.   Broken bones as a result of falls are more frequent than among youthful employees. Slower reaction time and lagging reflex action is observed among some individuals over forty-five; the delayed response may account for certain serious accidents among older workers.   Such information can be helpful when counseling older employees.   They can be guided into suitable jobs that match their physical capacities.

Social Security legislation, which makes retirement possible at the age of 65, has eliminated many of the former objections concerning the few working years of an employee before he is pensioned.   Employers pay only a percentage of retirement costs under Social Security.   Before this legislation was enacted, the employer paid the entire cost if his firm chose to sponsor a pension program.   Accident insurance costs where the accident rate has been high and the threat of increased premiums have been a deterring force which has held back the full utilization of this more stable work force in many communities.

> There are two major problems involving the aged worker: (1) the problem of the employer to find suitable jobs for his workers who have grown old in his services and who can no longer efficiently carry on their work in their accustomed occupations, and (2) the problem of the older worker who finds himself out of employment and is faced with opposition to re-employment because of his age.[4]

Some advocate using these men and women workers for sweepers, janitors, and general clean-up work. There are hazards involved in these jobs, however, that require greater agility and better eyesight than is possessed by older men and women. Janitorial work frequently places workers in the path of moving trucks and other plant vehicles; cleaning up around fast-moving machinery is not a safe answer to the problems of retaining older workers.

The desirability of using elderly men as night watchmen is another practice open to question. The elderly man who possibly may fall in the dark, or suffer a heart attack or paralytic seizure is obviously not suited to perform watchman's duties.

When an older skilled or semi-skilled employee must be taken off the production line for safety's sake, there are many material-salvage operations to which he may be assigned. Maintenance work that is not of a rapid production nature might well be considered for these workers, also.

The counselor will find it considerably more difficult to sell the idea of utilizing the skills of these older workers to management than it will be to get the older men to perform efficiently the tasks assigned them. The counselor should be alert at all times to the need for transfers within this group, and much persuasion may be

---

[4] Scott, Clothier, Mathewson, and Spriegel, *Personnel Management*. New York: McGraw-Hill Book Company, 1941.

necessary to convince the personnel manager, the department head and the supervisor that such changes are desirable. The counselor, with access to publications, reports, studies and other data on the satisfactory utilization of older employees, may present pertinent information to management when the matter of job classifications for this group is discussed.

Public Employment Office Counseling of Older Workers

The second counseling problem is that of unemployed older workers. The main responsibility here, of course, rests with the Public Employment Service. It is possible for all tools of the USES counseling program to be brought into play in placing increased numbers of older workers.[5] Tools at the disposal of USES counselors include:

1. Services of the training division
2. The community services directory
3. The Dictionary of Occupational Titles
4. Job families cards
5. Job analysis
6. Physical demands analysis
7. Industry composition pattern
8. Interviewing aids
9. Physical capacities appraisal
10. Job descriptions
11. Labor market information:
    a. Local industry facts
    b. Area statements
    c. Industry series
12. Reports from other Labor Department Services

The skills possessed by older workers were an asset during World War II and it was possible to employ these individuals in increasing numbers. In a period when labor is plentiful, however, placement of older workers is more difficult but no less important. While it is not to be expected that job placement of large numbers of older workers will continue indefinitely, it is to be hoped that employment counseling by Public Employment

---

[5] For a more complete definition of the term "employment counseling" read: Virginia Greenberg, "Employment Counseling of USES," *Manpower Review,* March. 1945, pages 5, 23-24.

Service workers will assist those older persons seriously in need of jobs.

Counseling Young People

In the matter of employment opportunities young people are searching for essentially the same things that make up the goals of attainment for the adult group.   But there is a difference: young people often have fewer facts and less experience than adults to contribute towards the solution of a given problem.[6]   Consequently, the counselor must explore—must probe deeper to determine just what information the young counselee has to contribute—before he attempts to draw conclusions or to suggest avenues leading to possible solutions of a given problem.

In young people, the desire to achieve the goal may be very intense, or again, it may be superficial.   Balance and stability may be as necessary to the counselee as some other qualities sought for in the adult group.   These vagaries make youth counseling interesting but tricky business.   Young people may have everything it takes to do a given piece of work or to succeed in a given undertaking, but if they lack a motive, they may fail completely.   On the other hand, a young person lacking such important measurable characteristics as training, experience, and judgment, may succeed through sheer determination and drive.

Counselors working in youth guidance are impressed with the fact that young people are usually more ready to accept suggestions and to try out new ideas than are adults.   This places added responsibility upon the counselor.   Youth counselors must continually guard against unduly influencing young people in a direction pleasing and satisfying to the adult, but inadequate or undesirable to the counselee.

It is well to keep clearly in mind that testing is still the most important factor in the scientific counseling of youth.   Tests give sound clues to what otherwise might remain hidden abilities and

---

[6] Donald G. Paterson, Gwendolen G. Schneidler, and Edmund G. Williamson, *Student Guidance Techniques,* pages 6-12, 302-304.   New York: McGraw-Hill Book Co., 1938.

interests. Moreover, batteries of tests give more reliable data upon which to base suggestions than do single tests, although we are still not certain that even the best tests in several fields measure exactly what they purport to measure. Brief testing periods and simple testing devices are less disconcerting to the counselee; where tests have reliability and validity, they are recommended for use in counseling.

A counselor not skilled in the technique of using standardized tests should find out from others in the field how certain tests have been used to best advantage. Counselors who feel unqualified to administer or interpret tests may request the plant management to hire psychologists to conduct the activity. Counselors have found tests valuable in the following situations:

1. For vocational and educational guidance purposes
2. For research and analysis purposes
3. To determine behavior traits
4. To measure various special abilities
5. To aid in job selection and placement
6. For job-adjustment and advancement purposes
7. For measurement purposes relating to an understanding of occupational and social relationships
8. To determine general intelligence.

Youth, like adults, craves recognition. Young people are constantly seeking to build self-confidence, a place in the world, and some degree of security, yet they are not always conscious of this fact. Youth counseling is largely a guidance function. The counselors most successful in guidance positions are those who have had wide and varied experience themselves, and who keep up-to-date on many subjects of a social and economic nature.

Clear-cut, accurate, occupational information is what our young people are seeking. A detailed history of an occupation may be helpful to the counselee in making his decision, but timing is of such vital importance that the counselor must furnish pertinent factual information on present-day job requirements and future undertakings.

There is growing difference of opinion as to the limits of a counselor's viewpoint. There are those who argue for a sharply limited horizon in youth counseling; others, with a wider vision, picture unlimited opportunities for our young people. An international outlook for counselors is highly desirable in a world made small by rapid transportation and communication. By way of caution, however, it is suggested that complete information on local jobs be obtained first, before a search is made in distant areas. Competent counselors with vision can then broaden their outlook, and thus strengthen their entire program. If the premise is accepted that the objective of all good counseling is to help the counselee to help himself, then the counselor's responsibility is to furnish young people with a clear understanding of the local employment opportunities. Assisting youth in selecting an occupation which will yield satisfaction is a serious counseling responsibility. The counselor himself needs a clear understanding of the varied aspirations of each young person he is attempting to serve.[7]

In counseling young people entering the labor market for the first time, the following steps should aid them in satisfactory job adjustment:

1. Help the individual define his problem.
2. Give suggestions for a plan of action based upon an evaluation of experience, potentialities, hobbies, abilities, and talents, as well as the results of general intelligence tests. Make full use of the aptitude testing services of the Public Employment Service.
3. Understand the training facilities available within the community and base suggestions upon ideas within the power of the individual to attain.
4. Have specific information available on job opportunities and employment trends within the community and the state.
5. Refer the youth to the agency you feel will do the most good in solving the problem confronting him. Send the coun-

---

[7] For a discussion of counseling techniques to be used where there has been no vocational choice on the part of the counselee read: E. G. Williamson, *How to Counsel Students*, pages 435-440. New York: McGraw-Hill Book Company, 1939.

selee to a specific person, make the necessary arrangements in advance. Follow-up to make certain the counselee arrives, has a successful interview, and receives help. Whenever possible "break the way" for the young person by having him contact people who will help him put his plans into effect.

6. Match interests, abilities, and known traits with job requirements whenever there is no previous experience upon which to base recommendations.

7. Try to discover whether failure to make adjustments in the past was the result of a weakness in the individual.

8. Get information concerning the employer's dislikes. Point out characteristics that may help the young worker make the necessary adjustment to these personnel policies and hiring practices.

9. If the counselee has weaknesses that retard his progress, assist him in discovering his weaknesses and explain ways in which he can overcome them.

10. Follow-up on all your young counselees to determine the effectiveness of your work.

11. Repeat any or all of the ten steps if there is a need for remedial treatment.

Single-Skilled Workers

Many patriotic Americans stopped their normal activities to join the great group that fought the war on the production line. Today they are classed as single-skilled workers with few job outlets. Some have returned to their usual work in the kitchen or on the farm, but many are in the labor market to stay. Economic conditions following the cessation of hostilities have been so favorable that the nation has not felt the full impact of this new group on the labor market.

Sooner or later, however, these individuals will be applying for work in sufficient numbers to create a counseling problem for the Public Employment Service and the interviewers of many plant personnel departments. What suggestions should be made to a young war widow who must support her child? She was a riveter in an aircraft plant during the peak production days, but is now unemployed. Does the answer to her problem lie in additional vocational training, a job as a waitress, in getting out of the labor market, or in trying to find employment that might use the skill she acquired during the war?

In the opinion of the authors, retraining at public expense should be available to former war workers, but few communities seem financially able to provide this service. The Veterans Administration provides funds for communities to establish vocational programs geared to the needs of service veterans. There is not an agency to pay the bills for former war workers, however; their retraining problems are not being met. Too few cities have trade and vocational schools that cater to adult groups; hence, an adult who might be interested in retraining will find that he must enter classes with youngsters or go without retraining. Many veterans found this condition when they enrolled at educational institutions. Gradually, there has been an awakening to the needs of veterans and they are somewhat belatedly being provided facilities in keeping with their age and capacity.

The skills of our people are a natural resource just as much as our forests, our iron mines, and our farm lands.[8] These abilities should be developed and broadened. The wise counselor, faced with the problem of helping a single-skilled person, should suggest the desirability of additional training and should be prepared to guide his counselees to the best available source for that training. Adults will frequently find that acquiring additional skills involves traveling several miles to a trade school, or joining a local union to benefit from its apprenticeship program. Such conditions are not always acceptable to all persons who want and need skills.

Men who are interested in developing added skills should investigate the possibilities of an apprenticeship. However, the ordinary civilian who has reached adulthood without military service will find that apprenticeship wages in many industries will not provide a basic living wage. Veterans will find this routine pretty well paved for them, and it is suggested that the counselor

[8] For additional information on skill as a resource, see: Virginia P. Robinson, *The Meaning of Skill*, pages 7-31. The University of Pennsylvania Press, 1942.

acquaint himself fully with the benefits of the apprenticeship plan. The Department of Labor apprenticeship representative in any locality can furnish all the necessary facts.

The problems of the single-skilled worker are not easily answered. Fortunately for us all, industrial activity following the war has held up remarkably well, thus postponing many contemplated placement problems. The Community Guidance Center or the Public Employment Service counselor can do no more than get the facts concerning the counselee, and, knowing community outlets, help the individual into retraining and re-employment. The matter of occupational composition studies used to determine the pattern of jobs required might well be carried out on a national basis to keep our supply of skilled workers equal to our emergency needs. Mass production techniques alone will not win the next war. It took time during the recent war to produce single-skilled workers. In an atomic age, the amount of time at our disposal for the training of skilled workers may be very brief. The alert counselor will want additional information on the technique of making an occupational composition study.[9]

Displaced Workers

Problems of single-skilled displaced workers are somewhat similar to those of the single-skilled in home communities. Displaced workers, however, are in the difficult position of being many miles away from home. Figures indicate that they use up their savings and unemployment compensation in a relatively short time and they become charges of the community of their adoption.

Our rapid transportation system makes it possible for skilled workers to move about the country in search of employment suited to their specific needs. Counselors will do well to check into the skills possessed by displaced workers. Multi-skilled workers should be retrained in the community, since the loss of

---

[9] Carroll L. Shartle, "Fitting Workers to Jobs," *Personnel Journal*, March, 1942, pages 328-332.

a good workman is a genuine loss to any plant and to the resources of the community as well.

The greatest movement of industrial workers has been from the Central States to our coastal cities of the West and South. Eighty-two metropolitan areas along these coasts gained almost four million people during the peak of war production. While the South and West gained most, the North, East, and Central states just about balanced loss against gain. Cities that gained in population secured some emergency war-housing to take care of the rapid expansion, but returning servicemen and an increasing birth rate have further aggravated the problems of these already overcrowded cities.[10] Many of these cities will have to expand further their housing, transportation, educational, recreational, and sanitary facilities. Expansion must also take place in many service fields; laundries, barber shops, bakeries, grocery stores, and other types of business establishments will be needed to handle the multiplied demands of an increasing population. The counselor should be aware of the situation in the area he serves.

The housing shortage of the nation is well known. Gaining entrance into the building trades is not an easy step, yet the door is not closed to many who are young of body and spirit. Displaced workers from our war industries may be readjusted to fit into the employment pattern of industrial cities that are badly in need of additional homes and the individuals to build them.

It has been pointed out by some that this transition to peacetime employment must be reasonably swift, because displaced war workers usually are mature individuals with family responsibilities. The latter absorb savings and unemployment benefits until an entire family may become the responsibility of the community.

---

[10] There will be much unrealistic thinking about employment, jobs, and owning a business in the years immediately following the war. This fact is clearly pointed out in the following article: Major S. H. Kraines, U. S. Medical Corps, "Industry's Role in the Readjustment of Returning Veterans," *Texas Personnel Review*, Vol. III, No. 4, pages 54-61.

Community guidance counselors frequently will have to make the decision as to whether or not industries of the surrounding area can employ the services of the displaced worker. Those who cannot hope to find employment nearby should be encouraged to utilize the facilities of the Public Employment Service in locating an area where their skills and abilities can be used to advantage. Some, perhaps, should be urged to leave the city and try farming. Additional training by our vocational schools is one of the best answers to the employment problems of young, old, displaced, and single-skilled unemployed citizens.

Displaced workers whose wartime jobs have been abolished may be classified by the counselor into three general groupings: (1) those who should be directed into existing jobs in the community; (2) those who should be retained and retrained by the community; (3) those who should be advised to return to their home communities.

Few counselors will need coaching as to which individuals should be placed in any one of the above-mentioned categories. Skilled workers are an economic asset in the community and should be retained if there is any possibility of their being used within a reasonable length of time. What is more, these workers are more easily retrained than are those with no skills whatsoever.

Women Employees

In today's industrial job organization the only work that a woman cannot do is one requiring heavy lifting, pulling or pushing. Possibly, we have looked overlong for the inequalities between the sexes rather than to the comparable qualities.[11] Time, and the experience of many employers, have proved that women are the equal of, or superior to, men in many production jobs.

Since women have long accepted the unprovable opinion that

---

[11] The introduction of great numbers of women into industry during the war period heightened the need for counseling. Ordway Tead, "Employee Counseling: A New Personnel Assignment—Its Status and Standards," *Advanced Management,* Quarterly Journal of the Society for the Advancement of Management, 29 West 39th Street, New York, July-September, 1943.

most skilled jobs require the superior intellect of the male, they have found it difficult to break down the wall of opposition to female employees in industrial plants. The feeling that most production work in the basic, heavy industries belongs to the men kept management on edge during the war period when, of necessity, women took over more and more of these jobs. The actual hostility of many men to the encroachment of women industrial workers made the job adjustment of some women difficult if not impossible.

Experience has indicated that where large numbers of women are employed, the presence of a counselor for every 150 to 300 women seems to be desirable. According to a study made by Helen Baker, "Three-quarters of the companies using counselors indicated that counseling is best done by a person of the same sex as the employee seeking help. In every instance in which counseling is available only for women employees, women counselors are utilized. About half of the companies providing counselors for all their workers have male counselors for men and female counselors for women."[12] There is evidence, however, to prove that some women prefer men counselors; and that men willingly call upon a woman counselor for advice. Much of the work in counseling women consists of preventive measures. The following suggestions are offered on how to build good work habits in women:

1. The new woman worker is just another worker—forget her sex—treat her as a worker—not as a woman.

2. Remember that technical terms which are the common vocabulary of most men are like a foreign language to most women.

3. Start at a low level of instruction. Do not assume that the woman has any mechanical knowledge or experience.

4. Repeat instructions the first few days to make sure that the basic instructions are clear and understood.

---

[12] Helen Baker, *Employee Counseling*, Industrial Relations Section, Department of Economics and Social Institutions. Princeton: Princeton University Press, 1944.

5. Explain operation of machines and handling of tools in simple, understandable language.

6. Women may be slow to learn at first but do not label them as "dumb." Give them a chance.

7. Stress terminology and nomenclature and help women build confidence so that they can master the subject.

8. Demonstrate how to do the job. Use the methods of instruction that have proved successful with men.

9. Enforce safety rules and regulations. You are more familiar with the hazards than the woman who has not worked in a shop.

10. The wise supervisor will inform the male workers in advance that women are to work in the department. He will give necessary explanations and will let the male workers know what is expected of them.

11. Do not seek the favor of women workers.

12. Women naturally prefer men supervisors. If you are smart you will maintain that favor by discretion and tact.

13. Do not reprimand workers in front of others or in a loud voice.

14. Require women to work in the same manner and under the same conditions as men. After all, they are paid employees and the job to be done is the same.

15. Do not pamper women any more than you would men.

16. Emphasize the need for giving a full day's work. Watch time lost!

17. Check your own personal appearance, attitude and habits.

18. Establish the feeling of friendliness but not of familiarity.

19. Do not play favorites.

20. Be patient—do not yell at a worker.

21. If you resent supervising women, they will be aware of it and you will be less successful.[13]

We are moving in the direction of the complete integration of women into the employment fields formerly considered open only to men. It remains to be seen what impact a period of economic

[13] "The Job of the Industrial Counselor for Women," Federal Security Agency, United States Office of Education, Vocational Training for War Production Workers. Washington: Superintendent of Documents, Government Printing Office, 1944.

stress will have towards retarding the progress made during World War II.[14] If the movement goes unchecked for the next fifty years, many liberal thinkers may be surprised with the progress made. Procedures have been pretty well established for women to enter, progress, and win promotion in industry. Counseling has contributed its share towards smoothing the way for women workers. With the rough spots eliminated, women will remain in all types of jobs and in all industries.

Questions

1. How should the technique of questioning be used in the counseling process?
2. What are some factors to consider when suggesting plans of action for the counselee?
3. What should the counselor know about the older worker when offering assistance?
4. List ten of the counseling tools used by the Public Employment Services.
5. What differences exist between older and younger persons of which the counselor must be aware?
6. Are tests of value? If so, how can the results be utilized?
7. What steps should the counselor take with persons who are entering the labor market for the first time? List ten.
8. Does the single-skilled worker have a problem? Does the employer have any responsibility in solving this problem? Discuss.
9. What are some of the problems of the displaced worker? How can the counselor help?
10. Discuss women in the labor force and the part the counselor can play in assisting with proper adjustment.

Bibliography

Beaumont, Henry, *The Psychology of Personnel,* pages 54-120. New York: Longmans, Green & Co., 1945.

---

[14] For an interesting treatise on women in a new field of personnel work read the bulletin prepared by the United States Department of Labor, Women's Bureau, Washington, D. C., "Women in Personnel and Industrial Relations Work in War Industries," March, 1943, pages 1-4, 7-8.

Gardner, Burleigh B., *Human Relations in Industry,* pages 263-271. Chicago: Richard D. Irwin, Inc., 1945.

Hildreth, Gertrude H., *A Bibliography of Mental Tests and Rating Scales.* New York: The Psychological Corporation, 1939.

Super, Donald E., *The Dynamics of Vocational Adjustment,* pages 18-28, 107, 245-246. New York: Harper & Brothers, 1942.

Employment Counseling Handbook for Kentucky. Prepared by Technical Services Division, USES, Frankfort, Kentucky, July, 1944.

How to Establish Counseling Services 7

THE number of human relations problems and the manner in which these problems are handled in an organization will indicate either the necessity or the lack of need for a counseling program. Counseling services are of little advantage unless they meet a well-established need. In situations where quantity and quality production are at a maximum, and labor turnover, absenteeism, and similar problems are at a minimum, it would seem that little demand exists for the services of a counselor. Few plants, however, possess such a record.

Should the time come when all employees make the best possible use of their training and experiences, and have acquired sufficient knowledge of human relationships to solve all their job problems, then the counseling need will have passed. At the present time, however, the need for better human relationships is very great. At this moment, many individuals and organizations are looking for ways and means to settle their present difficulties and to avoid similar problems in the future.[1]

The availability of well-qualified persons to do the counseling job is a consideration of great importance. Since there is no pool from which to select trained counselors, securing skilled individuals to fill assignments in the counseling field is difficult. Some institutions of higher learning have begun to offer courses helpful in preparing persons to assume the role of industrial counselors. Jobs in the latter field are highly specialized, and traditional courses in child guidance do not fill the bill. It is the opinion of those who have worked with adults that adult coun-

---

[1] Considerable confusion exists at this time over provisions of the Taft-Hartley Act. For an interpretation of some of the provisions, see: "ABC's of the New Labor Law," *Modern Industry*, August 15, 1947, pages 54-152.

seling will grow in the years ahead. If this is true, future demands will lead to an increasing number of courses in counseling.
The approach to the problem of adult counseling will present
some difficulties not now encountered in the courses designed for
the guidance of adolescents.

During the period from 1943 to 1945, at the request of certain
industries, short, intensive courses were given industrial counselors through the co-operative efforts of the Departments of Vocational Education in each state.[2]   Some units of work were given
by qualified representatives of the United States Office of Education.   Classes were held in the large industrial and shipbuilding
centers, and instruction was given on a conference basis with each
member of the group contributing to the program.[3]   Techniques
and methods were discussed and evaluated and helpful conclusions were drawn.

These conferences for counselors helped many individuals
clarify their thinking about employee problems and human relationships.   Conference leaders saw clearly the need for specialized training of an adult nature that would take counselors beyond
the ideology of their work and assist them in obtaining a coherent
picture of the complete counseling function.

The Counselor's Duties Defined

If the counselor's duties have not been clearly defined before
his employment, then one of his first assignments might well be
that of analyzing, listing, and obtaining management's approval
of the activities considered to be his duties in the organization.[4]

---

[2] Frances W. Trigg, "More Efficient Use of Women in Industry." Nashville:
Tennessee State Board for Vocational Education, 1944.

[3] As an emergency measure, many women counselors were trained through con-
ference procedures by the United States Office of Education. See: Frances W.
Trigg, "The Job of the Industrial Counselor for Women." Washington: Federal
Security Agency, U. S. Office of Education, Vocational Training for War Produc-
tion Workers. Washington: Superintendent of Documents, Government Printing
Office, 1944.

[4] For an interesting and instructive article on the functions of the counselor read:
William H. Kushnick, "A Guide to Personnel Counseling," *Personnel,* November,
1943, pages 139-153.   New York: American Management Association.

These vary greatly among plants of equal size, and between large and small organizations.   Skilled, versatile counselors have been known to function as assistant department heads, assistant supervisors, welfare workers, employment managers, personnel directors, financial experts, advisers, and guidance officers.   It is not unusual for a good counselor to be called "Mr. Anthony." Making oneself generally useful has merit if the secondary tasks do not overshadow the prime responsibilities of the counselor's job.

The counselor should become acquainted with all key individuals in the organization through a formal introduction by the person highest in authority.   Each person in the plant should be given a clear understanding of the counselor's function in the organization.   It is suggested that discussion meetings be held for the express purpose of clarifying relationships which should exist between the counselor, top management, middle management, and the employees.   Substituting bulletins, memoranda, and notices for these meetings is a waste of time and effort.   Only through frank, open discussion can doubt and friction be eliminated.   No stone should be left unturned in launching the program intelligently.   Time devoted to an explanation of the counseling services will avoid costly misunderstandings and delays.   Provision should be made for "question raising" by those who can profit most from using the counselor's services.   Unless relationships are clearly understood by all employees and the counseling function carefully defined, confusion may reduce or render impotent the full effectiveness of the program.

Our discussion of the R. H. Macy counseling program, as well as that of the Federal Security Agency and others, has indicated the value of counseling to an employer who desires harmonious working relationships in his organization.[5]   Those about to employ a counselor frequently ask the question: "What will the

[5] For a discussion of the value of the counselor to the employer, see: Nathaniel Cantor and John C. Bonning, "Functions of Personnel Counselors," *Personnel Journal,* September, 1944, pages 104-110.

counselor do?" Assigned counselor tasks that have yielded an excellent return on the employer's investment include:

1. Developing and documenting factual data that will assist management in policy-making
2. Assisting supervisors on all levels with their human relations problems
3. Assisting employees with job and occupational adjustment
4. Conducting orientation and induction programs
5. Making recommendations for improvements within the plant
6. Organizing and conducting group activities
7. Assisting employees with family adjustments
8. Offering guidance on educational and vocational testing, training, and opportunities
9. Assisting employees who have financial difficulties
10. Suggesting health programs
11. Assisting those in need of professional care for emotional disturbances, mental illnesses, or other defects
12. Aiding in the improvement of quality production through the control of absenteeism and turnover
13. Keeping records showing the services rendered in the counseling, placement, and personnel fields.

The counselor's duties and responsibilities are many and varied. Principally, he is busy keeping in balance the delicate personnel relationships of the plant. Such records as are kept should assist in eliminating existing mistakes in management policies. Thus it is that the counselor climbs the ladder to success by keeping his house and the organization in order. In so simple a matter as that of organizing and conducting group recreational activity, failure to take all details into account may result in failure. Plant X did not have a counselor, but the top management, recognizing that employee morale needed boosting, assigned a busy but popular foreman to the task of organizing some recreational activity. The foreman rounded up some equipment, rented a hall, and asked a clerk to post a notice scheduling certain departments to appear at the hall on specific days.   By the end of the first week, the foreman and management were pretty well discouraged.   About 5 per cent of the minimum number needed to operate the competitive games actually showed up.   The few men that turned out finally started a checker game or two while four girls played a few rubbers of bridge.   The well-equipped gymnasium stood idle through the week.   The disappointed plant officials then decided to find out why employees were not attracted to the program.   A careful analysis proved that there was a need for someone to make and supervise adequate plans that would:

1. Permit workers to participate in the planning of recreational activities
2. Provide favorable word-of-mouth publicity for the undertaking
3. Give workers an opportunity to manage the affair after it had been planned
4. Offer employees a maximum opportunity to participate with a minimum expenditure of time and money
5. Make the affair an employee-conceived undertaking free of any smack of paternalism on the part of management
6. Extend a friendly counseling hand when the need for such service was felt by the employee committees working on the project.

Later on, when a counselor had been employed, committees were set up, plans were made carefully, publicity was favorable and adequate, and a small program was launched that continued to grow and flourish.   When employees realized it was their program, participation was large, steady, and satisfying to employees and management alike.

How the Counselor Functions

As a Representative

The counselor represents top management in interpreting plant policies, rules, and regulations.   Being sold on the organization himself, he sells others. As a management representative, he should be the fountainhead of reliable information for those who are entitled to accurate facts and explanations.[6]

As an Assistant

The counselor should make recommendations, suggest activities, and establish standards of attainment in the field of human relations. Through constant improvement, a plant or an organization can acquire a reputation of being progressive. Regardless of the condition of the labor market, workers tend to gravitate to the plant where management is regarded as upright and progressive. The urge to be associated with a going concern is strong, and this urge can be utilized to build morale. The integrity of managements' representatives is the touchstone with which to gauge the desirability of the plant in which to work.

To create good morale among employees, a mutual feeling of respect must be built between employees and all levels of supervision and management. Too often management's attention has been more concerned with materials, machinery, and products, than with the feelings, thoughts and attitudes of the men and women who operate the machines. Various experiments have proved that the attitudes of the employees can make or break an establishment.

Many supervisors are experts in their technical knowledge of production. They deal well with problems closely related to the job, but a surprising number of foremen have difficulty with problems involving human relationships. The counselor assists management by answering questions on policy which need further amplification in everyday language, and by utilizing psychological principles known to get results with adult workers. Helping foremen and workers to interpret rules, regulations, and announce-

[6] C. Gilbert Wrenn, "Recent Research on Counseling," *The Vocational Guidance Journal,* May, 1939, pages 694-698. New York: The Vocational Guidance Association, Inc.

ments is an important part of the counselor's activity. It is assumed that much of this sort of assistance can be given as the counselor moves about the production floor.[7]

Without Authority

Counseling is a staff function which should reinforce and strengthen the position of all middle management including leadermen, foremen, supervisors, instructors, and others. The able counselor needs no authority of his own. *His job is to help others to help themselves.*

Without Criticism

Regardless of the situation, nothing is gained by sharing with the counselee unkind thoughts about others. There may be many instances where the counselee is absolutely right in making candid statements, but this does not license the counselor to express even one adverse criticism. Treatment must always be of a positive nature. The job of the counselor is to work with people; he must always strengthen, never weaken; add to, never detract from; deal with, never run away from, any situation. *Helpful suggestions presented in a convincing manner and designed to correct any given situation should be the goal of the counselor.* The manner of the counselor should be conducive to relaxation, friendliness, and quietness. There must be no hint of censorship, either for past happenings or future plans, to mar the flow of information from which the facts may be obtained. The experienced counselor becomes an artist in channeling questions and directing well-timed comments which will suggest, stimulate, and encourage the counselee. The counselor should be keenly aware of the counselee's reactions in order to make the greatest use of the all-important factor, good timing.

---

[7] A description of the counselor at work in the Hawthorne Plant of the Western Electric Company may be found in an article by W. J. Dickson: "Employee Education and Counseling Programs," *American Management Association Personnel Series,* Number 35, 1938, pages 4-19.

With Service to All

Occasionally, counselors will be tempted to criticize foremen, fellow workers, supervisors, top management, and others. If counselors will remember that "service" and constructive criticism are the keynotes of their jobs, success will be more easily attained. Everyone, from the highest official to the newest helper's helper, should feel the beneficial results of the counseling service. It is only when such relationships exist that the counselor can justify adequately his job with an organization.

There must be a well-developed understanding on the part of the counselor as to why individuals react and behave as they do. Frequently, probing is necessary to uncover hidden pressures being brought to bear on the individual by outside persons or groups. The counselor must know and apply techniques that lead to confidence-building, emotional stability, and social adequacy. A study of the fundamentals of psychology should lead to the realization of the different types of behavior patterns and mental reactions.[8] The bluffer, the braggart, the timid, the face-saver, and many others are identified and understood more easily when one has met them in professional study. The counselor learns how to "unbend" many of these warped personalities through testing, interviewing, and suggesting ways to overcome personality difficulties known to even the "lay-psychologist." One does not need a doctor's degree to handle certain types with ease and skill; however, an understanding of the rudiments of psychology is most helpful. Ability to read and understand the literature of psychology is essential to success on the counseling job.

Goodwill Must Be Maintained

Counselors should study the techniques involved in developing and maintaining goodwill. The establishment of good employee-

---

[8] Nathaniel Cantor, "What is a Normal Mind?" *Personnel Journal,* May, 1944, pages 2-10.

employer relationships and the strengthening of counselee-coun-
selor relationships is the first major task to be tackled when entering the employment of an organization. Only by discretion and
tact can goodwill be established and maintained. Diplomatic
grievance handling is a real challenge to all counselors. During
the past several years, industry has learned the importance of
employee goodwill. It is wise to maintain this goodwill at the
highest possible level. Production at maximum efficiency and
minimum cost is one of the important outgrowths of a good mental
attitude on the part of plant employees.

The Importance of Friendly Service

Friendliness without Familiarity

Friendliness is a basic factor in a good counseling program.
To be friendly without becoming familiar requires practice. The
proper dividing line is not easily understood nor easily defined
because it varies with individual cases. Some counselees delib-
erately attempt to become familiar in the hope that they may "get
by" with misconduct. Occasionally, workers try to promote pet
ideas or get around rules and regulations with a personal touch.
The counselor should sense these situations and remain friendly
but firm and professional.

Assistance in Making Decisions

The counselor should offer to aid the counselee in making a
better adjustment to his or her surroundings. He should open up
or point out the best possible avenues for action, and should offer
aid to the counselee in making wise decisions, but refrain from
making the actual choices. The counselee must make his own
choice and then feel free and independent to carry out his plan.
It is much too easy for the counselor to promote an undesirable
dependence. The more independence a counselee shows in carrying out a plan unaided, the more successful the counselor has
been.

Intelligent Interviewing

Helpful counselors keep in contact with satisfied counselees. Many of these contacts come about as a result of planned follow-up interviews. Some counselors believe their success is determined by how well the interviewing, testing, and guiding are conducted. All documented evidence in the counseling field stresses the importance of showing genuine interest in the counselee, his problems, and his needs. It is well for the counselor to keep within the bounds of the counseling function by listening patiently, absorbing the information, and striving diligently to get all the facts.[9] To dominate the conversation, argue the point, jump at conclusions, become overwrought, or to act preoccupied is to scuttle all counseling efforts.

Warnings

Do Not Assume Supervisory or Managerial Duties

In establishing a counseling program, it should be made clear to supervisors, foremen, and others in charge that the counselor will not assume the responsibilities of these positions. The hiring of a counselor adds a service employee who should aid management in the better performance of its all-important task— namely, maintaining good personnel relationships. The counselor should not, by word or action, convey the impression that the duties and responsibilities of other supervisors will be assumed. A counselor should be a specialist in human relations problems. There is enough important work to be done in aiding workers with their problems to prevent the wise counselor from encroaching on the responsibilities of others.

In all industrial counseling, there are a few red flags which should be heeded as danger signals. Line supervisors resent,

---

[9] How seriously do you take your profession? For an interesting answer to this question read: E. Van Norman Emery, M. D., "First Interviews as an Experiment in Human Relations," *Readings in Social Case Work,* New York School for Social Work Publications, Columbia University Press, 1940.

and rightfully so, any tampering with their authority or rights. The counselor must enhance the position of all supervisors and should not in any way detract from their duties. Employees frequently feel they must be careful what they say to counselors for fear it will be told to the wrong person and result in unfavorable reactions. *It is important for the counselor to realize that the confidence of every employee must be gained and kept!* Counselors should *not* be of the type that derives personal satisfaction from learning all details of employees' private lives. Personal confidences should not be encouraged. The most desirable situations are where no more information is obtained than can be used to solve the problem at hand. Management should not expect the counselor to carry tales.

Avoid Fault Finding

Continuous fault finding and reporting of inadequacies is not the main function of the counselor. By the same token, the counselor should be given freedom in working out counselee problems without discussing the faults and inadequacies of his clients with supervisors and managers. Under no circumstance should the counselor run down the management, nor should disparaging remarks be made about plant policies. Conditions needing corrective action should be handled with top management in an objective manner. Patience and firmness will usually prove to be virtues in these dealings.

Abandon Case History Records

Information given in confidence is betrayed when it becomes part of a written record. It should be remembered that individuals do not wish to be treated as *cases;* therefore, counselors should not indulge in the keeping of long involved *case histories.* When individuals seeking the help of a counselor need to be treated as cases, they should be referred to the proper authorities who maintain a staff of professionally trained case workers.

Counselees may be urged to discuss specific problems with

specialists in certain fields. Follow-up to make sure the counselee has obtained satisfaction should be well-timed. The confidential record files kept by the counselor should be changing constantly to keep them small, flexible, and cogent. The counselor will do well to develop a long memory and an abbreviated filing system, since the personnel department file should contain complete permanent data on all workers. The counselor's files should not duplicate the records kept by the personnel department.

Questions

1. Name the basic considerations in determining the need for employing a counselor.
2. What responsibility does management have in introducing the counseling program?
3. What warnings are given counselors?
4. When are the counselor's duties decided upon?
5. Prepare a list of duties for the counselor based upon ideas contained in this chapter.
6. How does the counselor function as a representative?
7. Whom does the counselor assist and why?
8. Does the counselor have authority?   Discuss.
9. Does the counselor have supervisory or managerial duties?   Discuss.

Bibliography

Baker, Helen, *Employee Counseling*. Princeton University Department of Economics and Social Institutions, Industrial Relations Section.   Princeton University Press, 1944.

Dresse, Mitchell, "Guiding Principles in the Development of an Employee Counseling Program," *Public Personnel Review*, July, 1942.

Eisler, H. E., "Personnel Counseling Obviously Needed," *Personnel Journal*, 1943.

Kushnick, W. H., "A Guide to Personnel Counseling," *Personnel*, November, 1943.

McMurry, R. N., *Handling Personality Adjustment in Industry*.   New York: Harper & Brothers, 1944.

Counseling: An Aid to Management   8

ALL counseling services should aid management through improved personnel relationships. Happy, satisfied employees with high morale are recognized as good producers. Those activities that contribute most towards improved worker satisfaction and morale are of greatest help to management. This chapter is given over to a discussion of several counseling activities that directly affect employees. The degree to which employees accept or reject the assistance offered by the counselor may affect management directly in the quantity and quality of goods produced or services rendered.

Inducting New Employees

Because personal and job adjustment problems affect production, assisting employees to make early and satisfactory adjustments is most desirable. Counselors, recognizing that first impressions are important, should greet workers warmly upon their arrival at the plant for the first day's work.[1] A friendly greeting given by someone genuinely interested in the welfare of workers helps to ease tension; getting off to a good start gives workers a sense of "belonging."

The induction process, one of the best devices to use in making workers feel at home, consists of a series of well-planned steps by which the counselor eases the transition of the employee from his

---

[1] The authors have felt that the induction or introduction process is rightly that of the counselor. This point of view is supported by the findings of Helen Baker, in *Employee Counseling*, page 29. Princeton University Department of Economics and Social Institutions, Industrial Relations Section. Princeton University Press, 1944.

former situation to his new place of employment. The early development of a wholesome relationship between the employee and the management is important. Counselors aware of the significance of the induction process in the development of the employee-employer relationships have been improving the technique over a period of years, so that it now includes the following well-defined steps:

1. *Planning.* The induction process should be so planned that one step follows quickly upon another. If employees are permitted to waste time or are required to wait in going from one phase of the induction program to the next, they are likely to gain the wrong impression of management's ability to plan. Little value will be placed upon time if an employee senses that leaders place no value upon it. Planning should eliminate delays.

2. *Explaining.* Explaining the over-all policies and customs of the plant should be done carefully. If the wages paid employees rank higher than the community average, inform employees of this fact thus making them glad that they have joined the organization. Every detail that affects the amount of money they will find in their pay envelopes should be explained. An illustrated booklet will be helpful to the worker when he explains his income to his wife at some later date.

3. *Selling.* Selling an employee on the merits of the company includes pointing out to him certain advantages in pay (vacations, relief periods, and the like should be included here), type of work done, and the human relationships that exist in the plant.[2] Sell him on the plant through courteous and efficient treatment, and practical use of his time. Convince him that he has chosen wisely a workplace where his efforts will be appreciated.

4. *Escorting.* Escorting a worker through the plant can serve a better purpose than going only from the main gate to the work station. During this trip the worker may be shown how his job fits into the whole production scheme. Although his hopes should

---

[2] Carolyn L. McGowan, "Counseling in Industry," *Social Service Review*, pages 135-137. Chicago: The University of Chicago Press, June, 1943.

not be raised too high, he may be shown steps of advancement and told the factors that enter into promotions within the department.

5. Showing. Showing an individual where to put his hat, coat, tools, and the like is appreciated because it creates the feeling of membership in the organization. The new worker should be shown where to obtain tools, supplies, food, drinking water, first-aid, information, and relief.

6. Introducing. Introducing the new worker should be a warm, friendly affair. Those to whom he should be introduced include the foreman, supervisor, medical department, payroll division, personnel department, and any other individuals with whom he is to have contact prior to starting actual work.

7. Informing. Informing an employee of the recognized channels of authority involves letting him know to whom he is responsible and the extent of authority of his supervisor. Usually the immediate supervisor gives all orders and is responsible for all work of those under his supervision. If this is not true, tell the worker whom he is to go to for help when problems arise on the job.

8. Following-up. Following-up on a worker within a specified time will provide information on the new employee's reactions during his first few days or weeks.

9. Conducting Follow-up Interviews. The first follow-up interview should take place during the first week of employment. It is important to make this interview pleasant and friendly. Make it positive, and give the new employee constructive information and suggestions. Be very careful to avoid suggesting any possible reason for his not being satisfied.[3] Review with him some of the highlights pointed out during the induction process. Help the employee to develop good work habits and a constructive work spirit; try to create a sense of "belonging" to a co-operative enterprise. The counselor should be definitely interested in how the individual will move forward in the new work environment in

---

[3] For a discussion of the term "rapport" see: Rollo May, *Suggestions to the Counselor.* Texas: The Hogg Foundation, University of Texas.

which he finds himself. Because much of the counselor's activities should be of a preventive nature, the follow-up at the end of the first week may reveal some of the important inner drives that result in certain outward behavior. A technique which seems to yield effective results in uncovering these urges, drives, and motives is interviewing.

The Interview

Interviewing, one of the important counseling techniques, is a skill that must be discovered, perfected, and polished. A variety of interview techniques can be developed. The following suggestions are given to furnish a better understanding of the fundamentals of interviewing:

1. Why do we interview an employee?

a. To get information   c. To adjust complaints
b. To give information   d. To observe the employee
     e. To establish friendly relationships.

2. Important factors involved in interviewing include diplomacy, tact, courtesy, wisdom, understanding. When applied to interviewing, these words have the following connotations:

Diplomacy in phrasing questions, timing remarks, and in managing the interview so that maximum advantages may be secured by both parties.

Tact in the general plan of approach, in what is said and done, in making comments, and in phrasing questions that are clearly understood yet do not imply an answer or reaction. Tactful interviewing requires the delicate perception to do and say the fitting thing at the proper time.

Courtesy in voice, facial expression, directness of speech and in all that builds respect and consideration for others. Courtesy helps the counselee respect himself and also to have respect for the counselor.

Wisdom in dealing with facts and sentiments and in using information to suggest possible solutions to the problem.

Understanding the real meaning of what is said, grasping the proper connotation, catching the significance, having the ability to comprehend and interpret the concepts of the counselee.

The purpose of the interview is not to pass judgment upon but to understand better the individual or the situation, and to offer several plans leading to the solution of the problem. When these plans are developed by the counselee with the assistance of the counselor, the probable results should be stated as well. The counselee makes his own choice of the specific plan he proposes to follow. Having information concerning the probable results of his action, the counselee is in a better position to make a wise choice. The plan of action decided upon should be the one the counselee feels is the best for *him* to follow.

Very satisfactory results have been obtained when using the following procedure in interviewing:

1. Greet the employee with a smile. Be sincere.
2. Give your undivided attention to what is being said. Do not interrupt. Listen!
3. Gather facts. Avoid opinions and judgments.
4. Keep a friendly relationship. Be cordial and objective. Do not argue.
5. Keep on the subject. Ask questions to guide the conversation back to the subject.
6. Allow sufficient time but do not dawdle.
7. See problems from the employee's point of view, but understand supervisor's position and strengthen it whenever possible.
8. Assist the employee in analyzing the problems and clarifying the available information. *Let worker make final decision.*
9. Keep within bounds of your own knowledge, experience, and defined responsibilities.
10. Maintain a courteous manner. Avoid expressions of critical attitude.
11. Ask good questions, not ones which can be answered by "yes" or "no." Be sure that the worker understands the questions. Questions that start with Why, What, Where, When and How require an explanation rather than just a "yes" or "no" answer.

12. Use care in dealing with touchy subjects.   Hold interviews in private.

The counselor should avoid:

1. Jumping at conclusions
2. Displaying authority
3. Diagnosing apparent traits
4. Subjective likes and dislikes
5. Generalizations
6. Giving advice or moral admonition
7. Implying answers to questions
8. Impertinence
9. Classifying people into types.

Counselors who like people usually become the most successful interviewers.[4]   When done successfully, interviewing becomes one of the most potent devices for getting all the facts.   Frequently, the interview includes not only a question and answer period, but also a period in which the counselor may observe the actions and reactions of the interviewee.

Securing Action on Minor Job Maladjustments

The counselor is in a strategic position to create employee interest and enthusiasm by showing him the importance of his job to the organization.   Workers want to feel that they have some special usefulness.   Each worker is entitled to treatment as an individual.   Where minor maladjustments are uncovered, the cause for failure to become adjusted may provide clues to corrective action which may prevent the recurrence of similar maladjustments in the future.   For example, the counselor may recommend lowering or heightening a stool or work bench; improving the lighting over a work bench; or he may assist supervisors in the reassignment of workers in cases where physical disability, personal differences, and other conditions indicate that a change is needed.

[4] The following article is suggested for the counselor who desires to do an outstanding job of interviewing: Frances Ferguson, "The Human Side of Interviewing," Proceedings, Twenty-seventh Annual Convention, International Association of Public Employment Services, April, 1939, pages 89-90.

Employees transferred from one department to another should be followed-up in the same manner as new employees. In situations where transfers or other adjustments demanded by the employee are not logical, he should be told promptly *why* such action is not possible. Prompt counselor action is important because workers "talk up" situations in which they feel a sense of dissatisfaction. Situations that tend to drag on usually reach the shop steward or plant grievance committee.

Assisting Supervisors with Preventive Measures

When an employee complains to the counselor about working conditions, the matter should be reviewed to determine the frequency of that type of complaint. If similar criticism has been leveled at conditions existing under a particular supervisor or foreman, plans should be worked out with that supervisor to overcome the conditions responsible for the complaints. Several workable plans should be available to the supervisor as a result of the counselor's experience in handling similar problems.

Not infrequently, basic plant policy is at fault when complaints come in from many sectors. The counselor is in a strategic position to recommend changes that will eliminate the source of irritation.[5] There should be no hesitancy in going up the line in the organization to overcome unfair practices or unjust policies. As a preventive measure, rules, regulations, and policies should be presented to employees in such a way that they feel a willingness to accept them, rather than a compulsion to do so. Prevention means overcoming in advance conditions which will result in dissatisfaction.

In situations where a supervisor is involved, he should be given an opportunity to resolve the problem himself. If the supervisor cannot make the necessary adjustment to correct the problem, it may be necessary for the counselor to take the matter to the

---

[5] For details of a plan where the supervisor introduces the employee to the new work situation and gives information about the company, read: "Introducing the New Employee to the Job," *Personnel*, pages 15-22. New York: American Management Association, July, 1943.

supervisor's immediate superior. A clear understanding of the organizational pattern of the plant is of prime importance to the counselor. Tact and coolness is important in cases of this kind if misunderstandings and recriminating discussions of personalities are to be avoided. All matters should be approached from the standpoint of *helping* the supervisor and the employee. If necessity demands going up the line, then the approach must be that of the greatest help to the entire organization, namely, preventing the recurrence of similar problems.

If the counselor is keen-eyed and alert, situations may be spotted and called to the attention of the supervisor before they reach serious proportions. The use of tact in making suggestions is important. Whether or not the supervisor acts upon the suggestions given should not cause the counselor undue concern. Foremen who understand human relationships and have been trained in job relations programs will usually recognize the value of helpful suggestions given in a sincere tactful manner. Should the supervisor be unwilling to co-operate, the counselor may go up the line to the next person in the organizational pattern.

Preventive work is of course most effective when supervisors recognize the value of helpful suggestions and the importance of timing. Counselors in plants and in agencies where supervisors receive no training in personnel relations should explore the possibilities of having instruction furnished at an early date. The counselor is part of a flying trouble-shooting squadron that can and should prevent grievances from occurring. Timing and prompt action are factors which must be considered if breakdowns in the plant's human relations are to be avoided.

Assisting Supervisors with Women Employees

Most women workers do not wish to be treated differently than male employees, but, like all employees, they do want to be treated as individuals. Women excel in most jobs requiring delicate operations, intricate assemblies, and similar undertakings where skill, precision, and manual dexterity are essential. Possibly the only place where women cannot equal the "stronger sex" is in lifting, pushing, and pulling heavy objects; some women need help in adjusting themselves to the presence of noise and whirring machinery. Supervisors should recognize that most women are fine employees.

Adequate induction helps the woman employee to feel that she can and will make the needed adjustment to factory work; orientation will speed her adjustment to the workplace and make her feel that she is an accepted member of a team. Women appreciate helpful suggestions on the following topics when they are offered in a friendly manner:

The day care of children	Whom to see when in difficulty on the job
Information on housing	
Leaves of absence	Whom to contact when in difficulty off the job
Vacation periods	
Rest periods	Insurance and medical benefits
When, where and how to report complaints	
What is expected of them on the job	Items that may be purchased through the plant

The counselor should assist supervisors in assuring women workers that they have a right to first-hand information on any problem confronting them. The strain of not knowing where to go for assistance when in difficulty may delay maximum production.

Counseling Employees upon the Request of Supervisors

Employees usually turn to their supervisor or foreman for help when confronted with production problems. These problems are usually handled easily as he is a specialist in matters pertaining to production. There are times, however, when employees have problems which involve factors about which the supervisor has little or no information. For this reason, the counselor should be in a position to answer any and all questions concerning rules, regulations, and policies of the organization. Should the question fall outside the field in which the counselor has information, he has more time for research on the problem than a supervisor who is responsible for production schedules. The counselor must watch for results to make sure that he furnished a satisfactory answer to the worker who raised the question. Sometimes the employee is referred to another person or an outside agency for the correct answer. Under conditions of this kind, the counselor should follow-up to make certain that the worker gets specific help. There should be no buck-passing, nor should the worker be made to feel that he has been sent on a wild goose chase. A timesaving device for both counselor and employee is a counselor's guidebook of persons and agencies that have specific information on subjects of interest to employees. With this aid, a telephone conversation can often clear up minor items in a few minutes. On matters of greater importance, conferences may be arranged by telephone and the interested parties brought together promptly.

When supervisors request help on workers' problems outside the field of production, the counseling program is functioning as it should.[6] If workers seek counseling assistance on problems of a production nature, the counselor should refer the matter back to the supervisor and follow-up to make certain that the employee received a satisfactory solution to his problem.

Good, friendly relations should exist between the counselor and all levels of supervision. A feeling of mutual trust and co-operative effort should be promoted between the production department and the personnel department. Through an intimate knowledge and analysis of the non-production problems confronting supervisors, many hidden causes for dissatisfaction can be brought to light. Understanding the underlying causes of dissatisfaction is the first step in establishing a procedure that will prevent the recurrence of these and similar problems.

---

[6] Helen Baker, *Employee Counseling,* pages 30-31. Princeton University Department of Economics and Social Institutions, Industrial Relations Section. Princeton University Press, 1944.

Conducting Exit Interviews

Tight labor markets have taught us much about the values of retaining workers. Labor legislation has taught us why we need concise, accurate information about workers before hiring and after firing. It is a fallacy to assume that exit interviews should be abandoned when the labor market is not tight. During the war emergency, the War Manpower Commission found that a poor reputation established when labor is plentiful may make production next to impossible during a tight labor market. Exit interviews conducted as soon as it is learned that a worker plans to leave may reveal practices that need correction. Whether replacement is or is not a difficult task, a plant should strive to retain the goodwill of the departing employee.

Employees leaving the company should be cleared through the personnel department where the exact reason for the severance is recorded in the words of the employee. If the services of an employee are so valuable that their loss would work a hardship upon the organization, attempts to sell the worker on remaining with the company are justified. Whenever possible, an appointment should be made in advance so that the counselor may be reasonably well-acquainted with the employment record of the individual being interviewed. Supervisors may make this appointment with the counselor as soon as they know of the worker's plans.

The chance of retaining an employee seems greater if an interview can be arranged for a time at least two weeks before the worker plans to leave the company. Seldom will a worker change his mind if the interview takes place on the day he plans to draw his final paycheck. How well the counselor succeeds in retaining an employee will depend upon how successful he is in winning the confidence of the employee and in getting at the real reasons for his leaving. Studies have revealed that employees tend to tell different stories about their reasons for leaving when interviewed several weeks after their departure from the plant. These studies tend to show that it is difficult to get at the real reasons for employees changing jobs. Any pattern or similarity evident in the reasons given should be brought to the attention of top management and utilized to establish corrective measures to reduce labor turnover.

Such factors as inadequate cafeteria facilities, improper lighting, poor ventilation, poor toilet facilities, an absence of many conveniences, and low pay can cause workers to leave the plant. Individuals who feel that their work does not challenge their best efforts may sometimes be retained by assigning them to jobs of greater responsibility with more pay; some potential supervisors have been discovered in this manner. The effects of poor or inadequate supervision have been revealed in exit interviews; however, the counselor is in a strategic position to inaugurate human relations training for supervisors to overcome the deficiencies revealed by the departing workers.

Assisting Supervisors in Accident Prevention

Accident prevention is obviously of prime importance to supervisors. Maximum production can be established only when safety is at its peak, and accidents involving lost time are at their lowest point. Counselors can help supervisors with the safety program in many ways. An important service can be rendered by including in the induction an explanation, or a safety film series, of the plant's general safety rules. Some counselors use a true-false quiz to test the employee's knowledge of simple safety rules explained during the induction program; a check of this kind helps to reduce or eliminate the misunderstandings that contribute to accidents. Where a plant does not have a regular safety engineer, the counselor may organize a committee, keep a record of accidents, and conduct discussion meetings on safety measures. A few additional suggestions to counselors are as follows:

> 1. Maintain a close working relationship with the safety engineer or the safety department of the plant.

2. If the plant lacks adequate safety equipment for its employees, assist foremen in selecting, requisitioning, and putting into service such equipment.

3. Be alert to unsafe practices and call the attention of the supervisor to employees failing to observe normal safety practices.

4. If you have responsibility for safety make sure your plant is a member of the National Safety Council. Utilize the material of the Council in the promotion of safety within the plant.

5. Keep your committees interested and active. Keep employees aware of plant progress in reducing accidents by posting the accident rate daily on a scoreboard.

6. Investigate accidents with the view towards reducing to a minimum the accident and severity rates within the plant.

Warnings to Counselors

1. Don't assume routine responsibility for checking time cards, leave slips, or production reports. If assuming these responsibilities aids in solving some personnel problem, accept them on a temporary basis only.

2. Don't mention names and places when reporting tendencies. Be impersonal. Have the facts, however, and produce them when the situation demands such action.

3. Don't exaggerate or underestimate when reporting or discussing situations or trends. Just state facts.

4. NEVER LET THE SUPERVISOR DOWN. Don't by action, word or facial expression weaken the supervisor's authority; always strengthen his position.

5. Don't take action. Assist the supervisor in deciding upon appropriate action.

6. Don't ignore any level of supervision. Follow proper channels of authority.

7. Don't argue. Listen, get the facts, weigh the situation from all angles, and then, by proper presentation, tell your viewpoint to the supervisor.

8. Don't blame. Give constructive suggestions for improvements.

9. Don't give the impression of being cocksure of yourself. If crowded for an answer, say, "This is my decision based upon the facts I now have, but my decision can be changed if the facts justify it."

10. Be open minded and willing to learn. Ask the supervisor for his advice frequently.

In order to attain a smooth-running organization management needs assistance in strengthening and clarifying its policies. When the reaction of employees toward policies and practices is presented to plant officials, many grievances can be corrected. Goodwill between employer and employee needs fostering in both business and industry. Progressive employers welcome suggestions that build and maintain good morale. They also recognize the need for continuous adjustment of human relations problems involved in plant production. The counselor must acquire the proper perspective in order to keep management informed of the needs and desires of employees. Management cannot always grant every wish, but it can make counter proposals timed with such nicety that they prevent certain difficulties from arising. "Feeling the workers' pulse" and creating harmonious human relations are the principal functions of the counselor; prevention and correction are the keynotes.

Questions

1. What are the main points to be covered in an induction program?
2. What are the values of a follow-up interview?
3. Why do we interview employees?
4. What is the procedure for interviewing employees? List eight suggestions.
5. List nine items to avoid while interviewing.
6. Tell how the counselor can assist the supervisor in preventing and solving human relations problems.
7. Why are exit interviews of value?
8. Why do some employees quit?

9. Should the counselor be interested in safety devices? Discuss the relationship between the safety director and the counselor.
10. List eight warnings and hints to counselors.

Bibliography

Court, A. T., and others, "Assimilating Women Workers—Reducing Absenteeism," page 35. Production Series No. 141, American Management Association, 1942.

Drake, C. A., "The Exit Interview as a Tool of Management," *Personnel*, May, 1942, pages 346-350.

Fite, H. A., "Case Study in Employee Morale," *Public Personnel Review*, April, 1941, pages 138-140.

Fry, J. H., "Orienting the New Worker," *Factory Management and Maintenance*, May, 1943, pages 99-104.

Giberson, L. G., "Personality Problems in the Office," *Personnel Journal*, January, 1943, pages 239-243.

Hibbs, Ray E., "Labor Turnover." Minneapolis, Minn.: North Star Woolen Mill Co.

Hoslett, S., "Counseling in a Quartermaster Depot," *Social Service Review*, 1943, pages 466-471.

Maxcy, E. C., "Understanding People in Work Relationships," *Personnel*, 1942, pages 371-376.

Silvers, C. W., "Talking It Over," *Personnel*, March, 1944, pages 330-339.

"Attack Turnover—Help Her Stay on the Job." Washington, D. C.: U. S. Department of Labor, Women's Bureau, 1944.

"Mechanics of the Exit Interview," U. S. War Department, Employee Relations Branch, Civilian Personnel Division. *Personnel*, January, 1944, pages 231-239.

THE first few weeks are usually critical ones for the new employee. It is a period of adjustment. The new worker is more or less gradually getting his bearings. If supervision is of high quality during this crucial period, the worker will be developing good work habits that are later to become valuable skills. Because the individual develops attitudes along with work habits and skills, his morale should be kept at a high level during the adjustment period.

The practice of dumping green workers onto an overworked or ill-tempered foreman is all too common and usually results in disillusionment and dissatisfaction for both. It is of vital importance, therefore, that supervision be adequate, understanding, and sincere. The counselor, through contact with the foreman and the worker, can learn the attitude of each toward the other. Some skillful guiding, suggesting, and maneuvering may be necessary to keep the adjustment process functioning harmoniously.

Employee Adjustment Techniques

Contacts made by the counselor are similar in nature to those made by a supervisor. While the counselor functions without authority, he must be a keen observer alert to situations which affect the human relationships within the department. He should know what to look for and should make a fair evaluation of all that he hears and sees.[1] Since there are no set measurements to

---

[1] Personality is a potent factor in the adjustment of workers to the employment situation. Ten distinct groupings into which most personality problems may be classified are discussed by Lydia G. Giberson, M. D., in "Personality Problems in the Office," *Personnel Journal,* January, 1943, pages 239-243.

be made, the counselor must learn to estimate rather accurately the degree to which the worker will eventually become adjusted to his work situation.[2]   A frank discussion of conditions too early in the breaking-in process may frighten the worker unduly, and cause him to imagine that he is failing.   Conversely, an interview too late in the breaking-in process may yield disproportionate results because the worker's attitudes are so firmly established. Because there are no specific measures of the degree to which a worker has attained complete job adjustment, the counselor must discuss some elements with the supervisor. These elements include:

1. Suitability of the Job

    a. Is the worker able to meet the physical, mental, and other requirements of the job?

    b. Is the final job in the promotional sequence within the worker's ability?

2. Personality Traits

    a. Does his work give evidence of thoroughness?

    b. What does the worker's time card reveal in terms of absence and tardiness?

    c. What evidence is there of growing loyalty?

    d. Does he get along well with others?

    e. Has there been any test of his honesty?

    f. Is he dependable?

3. Progress to Date

    a. What is the worker's estimate of his progress to date?

    b. What is the foreman's estimate?

    c. What has been done to reconcile any differences of opinion?

    d. Have you as a counselor any first-hand information which will help to reconcile any differences of opinion relative to the worker's progress to date?

Attention is called to the Employee Rating Sheet pages 128-129,

---

[2] Joseph Tiffin, *Industrial Psychology*, pages 313-338. New York: Prentice-Hall, Inc., 1943.

NAME .... BADGE .... ACTIVITY ....

CLASSIFICATION .... RATING PERIOD ENDED .... REGULAR RATING ....

TRANSFER RATING ....

RATING FACTORS

MONTHS ....

UNDER SUPERVISION FOR.	5 4 3 2 1	10 9 8 7 6	15 14 13 12 11	20 19 18 17 16	25 24 23 22 21	Score
KNOWLEDGE OF WORK Ability to plan, organize and delegate responsibilities. Understanding of Depot personnel policies and Depot regulations. Understands and uses effective methods of discipline. Technical knowledge and understanding of safety precautions. Ability to select right man for right job and properly assign efficiency marking. Ability to discharge training responsibilities and give effective orders.	Organization and plans (if any) require constant and close attention of superiors to avoid disruptions—responsibilities delegated and forgotten. Consistently permits policies and regulations to be violated because of personal ignorance or interpretation of same. Fails to discipline workers or uses harsh methods creating unsatisfactory results. Possesses scanty technical and safety information—just enough to get by. Worker qualifications not considered in assignments—ignorant of efficiency rating plan and assigns markings at random. Does not recognize training needs or responsibilities—orders frequently cause resentment, are misunderstood and unproductive of desired results.	Often needs help in planning and organizing. Responsibilities loosely delegated without adequate authority. Lax in interpreting policies and regulations—often is misinformed and gives misinterpretations. Has trouble keeping workers in line—disciplinary measures ignored. Dependent on others for technical and safety information. Assigns subordinates to jobs according to expediency and often fails to revise assignments when unsuitability is significant. "Guesses" in assigning efficiency marking. Takes sporadic interest in training, inclined to rely on workers absorbing necessary skills—takes too much for granted in giving orders—commands rather than requests.	Plans day by day as needs are recognized and revises work assignments to meet current demands. Seeks information on Depot policies and regulations as pertinent situations arise. Dependent upon authority of position and regulations to enforce discipline. Possesses limited technical knowledge and prescribed safety precautions—attempts to secure information as needed. Matches subordinates and jobs with limited knowledge of worker's experience or efficiency markings given only through trial and error. Takes sporadic interest in training, not usually well informed of status of training—orders often need to be repeated and clarified.	Develops plans and effects necessary changes in organization with minimum waste. Delegated responsibilities are "clear cut" and clearly explained. Currently informed of all policies and regulations and transmits same to subordinates. Discipline secured through close supervision and effective disciplinary measures when needed. Familiar with basic technical knowledge and safety measures when needed. Assigns workers on basis of experience and physical characteristics—conscientiously prepares efficiency markings. Personally supervises and meeting training requirements and meeting needs—gives clear orders and follows up to assure compliance.	Exhibits strong evidences of foresight in cooperative planning, explicitly defines the worker responsibilities and relationships. Thoroughly conversant with regulations and interprets them for maximum compliance. Maintains discipline through good leadership and promptly administers effective reprimands. Possesses extended technical and safety knowledge. Scientific analysis of worker qualifications for valid job placement—careful appraisal of performance to job requirements. Assumes responsibility for organized job training and personally assures that training is highly effective—regularly gets exact results required without repeating orders.	
	5 4 3 2 1	10 9 8 7 6	15 14 13 12 11	20 19 18 17 16	25 24 23 22 21	
QUALITY OF WORK Standard procedures for jobs and safety are established and followed. Reduction in waste. Inspection of work at regular intervals. Improves work methods. Promotes and recognizes high-grade workmanship.	Procedures for work and safety are vague and often violated by workers. Inconsiderate of damage and waste. Quality of workmanship not considered in the few and hurried inspections that are made. Refuses to try or adopt new methods that have not been a part of his previous experience or are not his own developments. Depends on superiors or inspectors to identify and reject low quality workmanship.	Wide variation in job and safety procedures within his unit—lacks uniformity. Waste and breakage exceeds recognized limits with considerable re-work. Inspections are spasmodic and infrequent. Reluctant to recognize improved work methods and make changes. Sacrifices quality workmanship for quantity production.	Uniform standards for work and safety are verbally established and minimum deviation maintained through close supervision. Waste kept within recognized limits. Makes intermittent inspections to maintain present standards of work flow. Recognized improvements are adopted. Satisfied with workmanship that meets recognized standards.	Job and safety standards are generally established. Minimum waste through close supervision. Inspections are frequent and purposeful. Critically reviews work methods and does some research for improvements. Exemplifies and sets high standards of workmanship for workers.	Standard procedures and safety precautions for all jobs are thoroughly developed, kept currently recorded and adhered to by all hands. Negligible waste maintained through close planning and resourceful salvaging. Regular inspections are rigid and promote higher quality. Constant improvement of job methods through analyses, study and by encouraging worker suggestions. Encourages, recognizes and gets highest grade workmanship.	

QUANTITY OF WORK

Production of maximum results on schedule. Good housekeeping. Reduction of absenteeism and tardiness. Proper use and care of machinery and equipment. Coordination of work with that of other jobs or units.

25 24 23 22 21	20 19 18 17 16	15 14 13 12 11	10 9 8 7 6	5 4 3 2 1
Regularly exceeds work schedules and at the same time maintains highest order of other supervisory responsibilities. Maintains model program for housekeeping, which results in consistently neat, clean and orderly machines, equipment and facilities. Absenteeism and tardiness of crew is negligible. Maintains peak efficiency of machines and equipment through enforcing proper operation and maintenance. Planned coordination of work results in maximum overall efficiency.	Maintains work goals with an even production pace. Frequent critical inspections and specialized assignments and results in everything being shipshape. Closely controls absenteeism and tardiness through carefully planned programs. Through frequent inspections, ascertains probable machine or equipment failures and remedies same. Effectively dovetails work with that of other jobs or units as situations arise.	Meets work schedules but has rush periods and lulls. Intermittent cleanup periods accomplishes favorable standards of overall housekeeping. Casual attention given to curtailing chronic absenteeism and tardiness. Alert to machine or equipment failures and recognizes and overcomes causes. Coordination of work meets requirements with some duplication of effort.	Gets work done at the expense of other supervisory responsibilities. Corrects or adjusts unfavorable housekeeping conditions after notification—personally performs cleanup work. Excessive absenteeism and tardiness not adequately curbed. Permits machines and equipment to be operated when faulty and fails to correct source of inefficiency. Work frequently delayed and "bottlenecks" occur as a result of inadequate coordination.	Fails to meet work requirements. Cluttered, disorganized condition of area, which restricts production and presents hazards, uncorrected after repeated warnings. No consideration given to attendance or punctuality of subordinates. Frequently fails to prevent or acknowledge misuse or breakage of equipment or machines. No consideration given to coordination of work with other programs or units.

ADAPTABILITY

Leadership and ability to gain and hold the confidence of his workers. Ability to fairly represent management to workers and workers to management. Detection and proper handling of grievances. Accepts and discharges responsibilities. Preparation and submission of reports and records on schedule. Cooperates with other supervisors and units.

25 24 23 22 21	20 19 18 17 16	15 14 13 12 11	10 9 8 7 6	5 4 3 2 1
Workers willfully respond to ideas and requests and support same as their own. "Goes to bat" for just requests of his workers and supports and effectively justifies policies, orders and regulations of the Depot. Recognizes sources and evidences of worker dissatisfaction and takes early steps toward adjustment. Reports and records accurate and on time. Goes out of way to accommodate requests of other supervisors or units.	Orders and assignments are accepted and workers recognize his judgment on all decisions pertaining to their work. Presents wishes of workers to "top side" and transmits answers to them. Listens sympathetically to dissatisfied workers and takes appropriate action. Carries out responsibilities as directed. Prepared and records standards as directed. Satisfies requests from other supervisors and units.	Orders and assignments passed on as received and compliance required. Channels of authority are followed by workers on problems requiring action. Gets action on routine requests of workers and mandatory compliance with rules and regulations. Workers' "gripes" are considered and sometimes referred to higher levels of supervision for adjustment. Reacts to basic responsibilities and discharges them according to explicit instructions. Occasional prompting or revision of records and reports. Reciprocates for cooperation received from other supervisors.	Commands and threatens workers. Workers question his ability and sincerity and sometimes by-pass him with requests. Discourages requests from workers and evidences dissatisfaction with regulations. Resents problems of workers and makes false promises to evade difficult settlement. Resents some responsibilities and reluctantly discharges them. Must be "prodded" for reports that are incomplete or inaccurate. An individualist, cooperates with others when necessary.	"Drives" and "nags" workers. Arouses antagonism and is frequently by-passed. Workers' requests are ignored and rules and regulations are resented by him and his workers. Evades workers' grievances and permits grievance to reach stage of forced settlement. Shirks responsibilities and must be given simple, detailed, and often repeated instructions. Records and reports consistently overdue or inaccurate. Constant friction with other supervisors or units.

Position in Group		Position in Activity		Rated by:
Size of Group		Size of Activity Group		Reviewed by:

Total Score

(REMARKS TO SUBSTANTIATE RATING ON BACK OF SHEET.)

EMPLOYEE RATING SCALE DESIGNED TO ASSIST THE SUPERVISOR IN MORE OBJECTIVELY EVALUATING PERFORMANCE ON THE JOB.

Prepared by Mrs. Frances T. Dawson.

which may be used to chart employee progress. Circles drawn around the figures indicate the scores assigned to the employee. By connecting these circles with a series of straight lines, a graph is made which gives a quick, visual comparison with the scores made on former periodic ratings; it may also be compared with the ratings assigned to an employee by other supervisory employees.

4. Future Plans

a. Does the evidence at hand indicate the worker has made a complete adjustment to his new work situation?

b. When do you plan to make your next contact?

c. What action do you plan to take when making the next contact?

Answers to these and other questions help to inform the counselor as to the extent of the employee's adjustment. In order to interpret the data adequately, the counselor must be fully acquainted with the plant and the activities of its supervisory staff. This acquaintanceship can only be attained through face to face contacts. It is recommended that where the counselor has not become thoroughly acquainted with personnel policies and conditions within the employing plant he learn about the possible adjustment impediments in the following manner:

1. Obtain permission from top management to study working conditions and job types through a brief on-the-job work-out in each plant department.

2. If actual experience cannot be gained in the manner just suggested, the counselor should utilize definite periods for observation "on the line" or on the production floor.

3. Study the job descriptions and specifications of all key or skilled jobs. After these are mastered, review the requirements of lesser jobs.

4. Study personnel records and compile statistical data on the following as time will permit:

a. What is the average age of the present work force?

b. Is the average age increasing or decreasing?

c. If there have been marked changes in these figures in recent years, call their implications to management's attention.

d. What is the ratio of men to women in the plant?

e. Is the present ratio considered ideal for the industry?

f. How does the turnover rate compare with other industries in the community?

g. Is the absenteeism rate considered good?

h. How does the accident rate of new workers compare with that of the plant as a whole?

i. Do the figures indicate a need for more careful induction and orientation?

j. How do employees rate the plant as a place to work?

k. Have workers been polled on their reaction to personnel practices?

Data on other pertinent questions should be collected to give the counselor an insight into factors that make the plant a good place to work and its employees a satisfied group, or that show the plant needs an awakened consciousness of the importance of good personnel relations and improved supervision. Management recognizes that there are inner drives that need satisfaction and that out of the failure to gain this satisfaction grows much industrial unrest.[3]

Aptitude, personality, and intelligence tests are helpful in placing workers in jobs for which they are best suited and to which they can become well-adjusted. A study of medical reports prepared when the physical examination is given often reveals information that is helpful to the counselor in working out adjustment problems.

Interpreting Rules, Regulations, and Policies

Few employees have the capacity to recall all the information furnished during the induction. To offset this common weakness,

---

[3] A psychiatrist's viewpoint on this subject is interesting. See: Lydia G. Giberson, M.D., "Psychiatry in Personnel Work," *Personnel Administration,* February, 1943, pages 3-6.

many plants supply small employee handbooks in which clever illustrations stress the importance of printed rules and regulations. Counselors should not assume, however, that handbooks, films or posters can substitute for necessary and desirable personal contacts with employees. The counselor should furnish explanations, and if necessary cite examples to clarify the meaning of plant policies. Telling a worker WHY a rule is necessary will do much towards overcoming forgetfulness and laxness.

The counselor can collect records of accidents, quits and work stoppages that resulted from failure to observe routine plant rules and regulations. Frequently, a mere recitation of the facts is sufficient to fix the material in the mind of an employee. Printed and illustrated posters placed at strategic locations throughout the plant tend to eliminate the alibi of forgetfulness. Noon hour movies on safety and social topics also serve to remind employees of safety measures and goals. Foremen, too, will usually appreciate all the help counselors can give them in putting across the real meaning of plant rules.

Frequently, "factory-born habits" such as smoking in the boiler room in a plant where no smoking signs abound supersede published rules. Counselors should suggest that such unenforceable rules and regulations be abolished, since blind adherence to them tends to weaken the entire disciplinary structure. It leads to distrust and disrespect for all law and order regardless of the reasonableness of the rule. In many instances, measures to eliminate outmoded rules and regulations are undertaken at once when the attention of management is focused on them. Such rules may be replaced, if necessary, with regulations that can be explained in terms of worker well-being. As a starting point for the framing of rules and regulations that are easily explained in terms of the individual's welfare, the counselor may begin with the problem of employee safety.

With the welfare of the employee in mind and with a committee drawn from among the various departments of the plant, the workers themselves can assist in formulating desirable regulations.

Rules worked out on this basis need little selling.   Management permission would, of course, be necessary for the counselor to develop a project of this kind.   The fundamental desire "to belong" can be satisfied through the introduction of an increasing amount of teamwork on the part of the employees.   The effect of this teamwork is reflected in the morale of plant workers.[4] Until management does feel the need for employee-developed rules, the counselor will do well to interpret present rules, regulations, and policies concisely, consistently, and fairly.

Be an Established, Reliable Source of Information

Rumors spread rapidly in most plants.   Thousands of man-hours of work are wasted daily as news of a proposed raise or cut, an impending shutdown, or a paid vacation makes the rounds. Many rumors stem from sources more reliable and nearer the top than do the denials thrown out to counteract the supposedly false information.   The family relationships of key policy-making personnel to subordinate employees should be investigated as the possible source of many plant rumors.   Leaks frequently occur in the main office where brothers, sisters, husbands, and wives pass the news—good or bad—down to someone who might be affected by the outcome.   Leaks of this kind start rumors circulating throughout the plant hours or even days ahead of the posting of a notice.   News of a pay increase is frequently common knowledge throughout a plant long before management has made up its mind how much of a raise it can or will grant.   If rumors are prevalent, persistent, and partially true, look to family-office relationships for a possible answer.   Many interesting combinations may be found.   Tracking down the source of plant leaks is interesting and challenging work.

It should be patent to those handling industrial relations problems that in the handing down of information from one worker

---

[4] Meyer Brown, M.D., Ph.D., *Morale in Industry as Seen by a Neuropsychiatrist,* pages 8-9.   Chicago: Industrial Welfare Department, Zurich Insurance Companies, 1944.

to another any facts very quickly become distorted. Distortion usually comes from flights of fancy engaged in by those repeating the original story. Individuals who pass on confidential information should be cautioned. They should be summarily dismissed if they persist in following this type of unethical practice and the counselor may be the one to make such recommendation based on the facts in the situation. Leaks in factual information should not be permitted to recur. When a true story gets started in the plant ahead of a genuine announcement, every effort should be made to present the facts to employees at the earliest possible moment. The regular channels for making announcements should be used to clarify the situation for plant employees.

Gossip can have far-reaching and disastrous effects upon the lives of workers. It is the source of much unhappiness, lowered morale, and employee dissatisfaction. Counselors have a responsibility to management and workers alike in the prevention and curbing of all types of gossip. Factual information about the plant and its operations can and should be printed in local newspapers. The plant magazine or house organ may be used as a means of telling management's story of plans or projected undertakings.[5] Newspaper editors are usually willing and anxious to get factual material upon which to base a news story on industrial development. The granting of pay raises, vacations with pay, or other worker concessions make good news stories and will be helpful if timed well with plant announcements.

An accurately told story in the plant magazine can do much towards dispelling many unfounded fears based on false rumors. Some editors make it a point to mail the house organ to the wives of workers. To increase the housewife's interest in the magazine, certain articles and pages are devoted to topics that would appeal to feminine readers. Plant policies, rules and regulations may be

---

[5] Keeping employees informed is a strong morale building factor. Meyer Brown, M.D., Ph.D., *Morale in Industry as Seen by a Neuropsychiatrist*, pages 25-26. Chicago: Industrial Welfare Department, Zurich Insurance Companies, 1944.

clarified on adjoining pages in a manner that is understandable and accurate. This method of handling factual material tends to dampen much harmful gossip; it tends to stabilize the working force by explaining the reasons for many of management's decisions.

Foremen, above all others, should be conscious of the fact that as rumors and gossip increase, production decreases. The counselor is in a strategic position at supervisory meetings to drive home these points on the prevention of gossip. Constructive criticism, properly timed and well-directed will do much towards eliminating conditions that breed gossip. Given the facts by management, foremen can assist in counteracting stories that are untrue, unjust, and unkind. Foremen should be sold on the plant in which they work, and should feel so situated in the management structure that they have only praise or constructive criticism for those above and around them. It is recognized that this condition borders on Utopia, but when gossip is involved anything less costs management more than the adjustments necessary to make foremen feel this way.

The counselor should furnish only information that can and will be backed up. Anything less is beneath the dignity of his job. The facts should always be brought out into the open and lies burned to the ground. If the mistakes are those of management, and some will be, the counselor should urge a frank admission of the error. Nothing is ever gained by hoping that the incident will blow over. Usually the thing that blows over first is worker morale. Weakened morale is always reflected in lowered production, increased absenteeism, and accelerated turnover.

The counselor should be the fountainhead of reliable information. He should establish a reputation for "square shooting" with those who come to him for an honest answer. It has been said that the best way to kill a lie is to expose it to the truth. Employers have found that accurate information given out by counselors tends to add stability to a program of improved industrial relations.[6]   Those who come to the counselor for information and interpretation should be given an honest answer in language they can understand.   They must be given facts that will stand up if the worker chooses to go up the line to a higher source for further interpretation.

The passing out of factual information has a lighter side as well; rules and regulations are not the only items on which employees seek clarification.   They frequently need help with income tax deductions, feeding formulas for babies, and the repayment of loans.   The counselor may not feel like keeping a straight face while listening to some humorous tale, but any signs of inattention or boredom will have a marked effect upon future worker relations.   Being gracious is as important as being reliable.

Counseling for Job Adjustment

It is fortunate, indeed, for the financial records of some managements, that we have no accurate estimate of the dollar value of time lost through inadequate worker adjustment to assigned jobs.   There is beginning to be a realization among personnel managers that individuals who become malcontent, prone to repeated accidents, or unduly irritable are probably not suited to the work they have been assigned.   More investigation along the lines of employee background, educational preparation and previous experience, and emotional stability is seriously needed. There is a need for a clearer understanding of the individual's ability to get along with others than is demonstrated in the congenial atmosphere of the brief employment interview.

Testing techniques are constantly being improved,[7] and it is

---

[6] For a report on employer experiences with the counselor as an informational service for employees see: Helen Baker, *Employee Counseling,* pages 18-22.   Industrial Relations Section, Department of Economics and Social Institutions, Princeton University, Princeton, N. J., 1944.

[7] For a comprehensive discussion of tests used in industry see: Joseph Tiffin, *Industrial Psychology,* pages 20-47.   New York: Prentice-Hall, Inc., 1943.

to be hoped that within a reasonable length of time we will have available to industry tests that will reliably measure the capacity of a worker to make the necessary adjustments to the job and to fellow workers.[8]   At present there are tests to record proficiency in arithmetic, reading, and language, but measurements of mechanical aptitude and manual dexterity are somewhat less accurate.   Some personality traits seem to be measurable.   Bona fide authorities on testing seem less certain as to the widespread application of their techniques to industry than are the pseudo "test experts."

Counselors not acquainted with the newer developments in testing should consult their public libraries; universities can sometimes mail additional up-to-date literature from their loan libraries if asked to do so.

Where a plant cannot or will not support a broad testing program, the counselor can make use of the application blank and the interview to investigate the statements of the applicant.   Interviews can be utilized to uncover hidden urges and drives that motivate individuals.   The hobbies of a worker may give satisfactory clues to the kind of work the individual could and would do if he could make his own choice of an occupation.   Research and reasoning of this kind might be pursued to a point where better worker adjustment would become the rule rather than the exception.

Obviously every employee cannot be transferred immediately when it is discovered that he is not satisfactorily adjusted to the job.   Careful selection and placement of workers may be considered as a preventive measure while the transfer procedure is, at best, corrective.[9]   Better selection can be made only when ac-

---

[8] For a discussion of the use of test results and other modern job placement techniques read: Perry Faulkner, "Nothing Short of an Effective Job Counseling Service Will Satisfy," *Manpower Review,* March, 1945, page 11.

[9] Additional information on selection may be found in: Dale Yoder, Ph.D., *Personnel and Labor Relations,* pages 136-143.   New York: Prentice-Hall, Inc., 1938.

curate job descriptions are available to personnel workers. Much rule-of-thumb personnel work will have to be eliminated before the number of poorly adjusted workers is noticeably decreased.[10]

A counseling program should serve as an adjustment device which helps workers develop a wholesome attitude while developing skill on the job. Listed below are the counseling techniques that lead to improved occupational adjustment.

1. The Counselor Improves Employee Adjustment to the Job by:

    a. Clarification of plant rules, regulations, and policies

    b. Interpretation of employee reaction to policies, rules, and regulations for management

    c. Promotion of a goodwill attitude on the part of management towards its employees

    d. Recognition of the human factors involved in production

    e. Promotion of programs to reduce worker fatigue

    f. Suggestion of ways and means to build and maintain worker morale at the highest possible level throughout the plant.

2. The Counselor Implements Improved Worker Adjustment by:

    a. Outlining definite plans for the improvement of worker-supervisor relationships

    b. Eliminating or reducing irregular attendance or late arrivals

    c. Suggesting changes in any conditions that tend to impede production

    d. Indicating improvements in heating, lighting, ventilating, and other physical working conditions.

3. The Counselor Keeps Management Informed of Progress by:

    a. Keeping adequate records that are readily available

    b. Making periodic reports to management.

---

[10] See: Meyer Brown, M.D., Ph.D., "What the Employer Can Do About His Employees," *Morale In Industry as Seen by a Neuropsychiatrist*, pages 17-18. Chicago: Industrial Welfare Department, Zurich Insurance Companies, 1944.

Performing Liaison Functions

The primary responsibility of production supervisors is the maintenance of acceptable production standards. Conscientious supervisors are frequently so engrossed in their problems that they appear to have little time to listen to gripes, additional troubles, and, in the hurley-burley of getting the job done, many workers hesitate to mention personal problems to their supervisor.

The counselor's prime responsibility is to lend an attentive, friendly ear to those who have problems. Situations needing adjustment can be called to the attention of the supervisor or to higher-ups, and improved conditions can be the rule rather than the exception. Through this close coupling of the worker and the management, better industrial relations may be realized more quickly.

Suggestions will frequently come to the counselor from workers who do not desire to use the regular suggestion system in vogue in the plant. These suggestions, if they relate to existing conditions, should be acted upon promptly. Prompt adoption of good, workable suggestions is an employee morale booster and is an excellent preventive for future complaints.

Some Counseling Precepts

1. Become friendly; don't become familiar.
2. Strengthen the supervisor's position; never weaken it.
3. Be fair with all employees; don't become involved in cliques.
4. Be quiet and unassuming; don't take on a supervisory air.
5. Give constructive suggestions; don't take sides in personal disputes.
6. Review your program frequently; don't continue to narrow your activities.
7. Publicize the truth; don't gossip.
8. Get at facts; don't jump to conclusions.
9. Suggest possible avenues; don't impose your opinion.
10. Be kindly and patient; don't fly off the handle.

11. Make few promises; don't fail to keep those you make.

The counselor, the liaison member of the personnel department, reaches into all departments, branches, and activities of the plant. Outcomes of a well-run counseling program include the following:

1. Employee efficiency is increased through better job adjustment.
2. Supervisors more nearly meet production goals because they are freed of many unrelated human relations problems.
3. Worker morale—the key to production—remains highest where workers feel management is interested in their welfare.

The counselor more than any other person can assist workers to become adjusted through interpreting in an unbiased manner the declared or implied goals of management.[11]

Questions

1. From the standpoint of management why are the first few days or weeks important to the worker?
2. Name and discuss the four job adjustment elements that are of concern to the counselor when a new employee reports to work.
3. Why are employee handbooks considered valuable to employees?
4. How should the counselor deal with plant rumors?
5. How can the counselor use tests? Are tests valuable in job adjustment? Are reliable and valid tests available?
6. What techniques of counseling may be used to improve occupational adjustment? Discuss.
7. In what way can the counselor perform liaison functions?
8. How can the counselor combat gossip?
9. List ten counseling precepts.
10. What are three outgrowths of a counseling program?

Bibliography

Bingham, W. V., *Aptitudes and Aptitude Testing.* New York: Harper & Brothers, 1937.

[11] Mary Palevsky, "How Effective Is Management Counseling?" *Counseling Services for Industrial Workers,* pages 16-17. New York: Family Service Association of America.

Broadley, M. E., *Square Pegs in Square Holes.* New York: Doubleday Doran & Company, Inc., 1943.

Carter, H. D., *Vocational Interests and Job Orientation.* Stanford, Calif.: Stanford University Press, 1944.

Drake, C. A., *Personnel Selection by Standard Job Tests.* New York: McGraw-Hill Book Co., 1942.

Heyel, Carl, *How to Create Job Enthusiasm.* New York: McGraw-Hill Book Co., 1942.

Hoppock, R. and Odom, C. L., "Job Satisfaction," *Occupations,* October, 1940, pages 25-28.

Hoppock, R. and Shaffer, R. H., "Job Satisfaction: Researches and Opinions of 1940-1941," *Occupations,* February, 1943, pages 457-463.

Lurie, W. A., "The Concept of Occupational Adjustment," *Educational Psychological Measurement,* January, 1942, pages 3-14.

Siedman, J. M. and Watson, G., "Satisfactions in Work," *Journal of Consulting Psychology,* July-Aug., 1940, pages 117-120.

Counseling:

An Aid to Union Welfare Activity   10

DEALING in legalistic phraseology rather than in human values has caused much distrust to arise between production workers and members of the personnel departments in many plants. Lawyers have too frequently been called upon to interpret and phrase labor-management agreements. Strict adherence to the letter of agreements made by those of a legal turn of mind has embittered many sincere union men. Employees' feeling of distrust for the personnel department because it represents management reflects these bitter experiences, and the counselor has to work diligently to overcome the suspicion and animosity he may find exhibited towards him and his work. It is not uncommon for the counselor to be completely ignored by those in key union positions.[1]

> In general, trade union leaders appear to have given little consideration to the development of employee counseling. The comments secured from union officers . . . seemed to reflect the attitude of individual union members toward the service rather than an official policy. Two union officers expressed the fear that the counselor might be used as an instrument of anti-unionism and to displace union activities. An article in the periodical of another union denounced counselors for mak-

---

[1] The authors, recognizing the feeling of union leaders towards personnel department workers, believe that counseling and training services can function most effectively when attached to the production division in the organization. Because personnel workers do not universally accept this point of view, it has not been emphasized throughout our book. Progressive managements might do well to give counseling and training an opportunity to function unattached to the personnel or industrial relations departments. In such a setup, these departmental heads would report directly to top management.

ing unfair and biased decisions. Moreover, both local union officers and personnel executives reported a cooperative attitude on the part of unions towards counseling where union-management relations were amicable. One union newspaper referred favorably to the counseling service in one company, telling of specific ways in which the service could help members and shop stewards.[2]

In principle, organized labor is opposed to management-sponsored counseling because of its belief that it connotes a regression to paternalism, it retards the maturation of workers as citizens, it is anti-union in its deepest essence. However, labor feels that a truly confidential relationship between the management counselor and the worker is difficult, if not impossible, to achieve. Living as he does in the perpetual shadow of job insecurity, the worker feels that if he gives the employer's representative information about personal weaknesses, it may be used against him when lay-off or staff reduction becomes necessary.[3]

It appears that where labor and management are genuinely interested in the welfare of workers and constituents, company-sponsored counseling can help those in need. A willingness to work co-operatively must exist between employer and employee if management-sponsored counseling is to be successful upon inception. Where good worker-management relationships do not exist, there must of necessity be a period of sparring until trust and mutual understanding can be built up. Only the strong counselor can rebuild from a position of distrust and suspicion.

During this period, management attempts at paternalism will meet with rebuff and an overzealousness may result in a request for the withdrawal of the program by union officials. The wise counselor will render such service as he is called upon to deliver.

---

[2] While this reflects the attitude of trade union leaders prior to 1944, a change toward a more receptive viewpoint is evident today. Members of the Princeton University Staff are as aware of the new attitude as they were alert to the skepticism of the earlier period. Helen Baker, *Employee Counseling*, page 39. Industrial Relations Section, Department of Economics and Social Institutions, Princeton University, Princeton, N. J., 1944.

[3] Mary Palevsky, "The Union Counsels Industrial Workers," *Counseling Services for Industrial Workers*, page 35. New York: Family Service Association of America.

Building goodwill without giving the impression of prying into
union activity or forcing counseling services on employees will
assist in moving the program through the troubled waters where
management and union representatives maintain a "stand-offish"
attitude towards each other.

Cantor has this to say about the counseling program in relation
to the union:

> The counseling service must be so defined that at no point
> does it violate any provision of the collective-bargaining agree-
> ment in existence at the plant. It should in no way interfere
> with the management-union machinery for dealing with griev-
> ances. Local union representatives sometimes express fear
> that the counselor movement could be used as an instrument
> to supplant the union benefits and interfere with union activi-
> ties. In some cases, shop stewards may complain that the con-
> sultant can only represent management's and not labor's point
> of view, and hence the movement should be closely watched.
> If the supervisor or head of the counseling program is clear
> about the purposes of the program, it should be a relatively
> simple matter to explain such misunderstandings or failures
> to understand.[4]

Frequently, however, the matter of explaining away misunderstandings is not possible with the simple wave of one's hand.

The following passages from *Counseling Services for Industrial
Workers*[5] describe recent efforts of union members to organize
counseling services:

> It was only yesterday that he (the union member) dismissed
> them (the social workers) with a contemptuous wave of the
> hand, as the boss's stooge hired to scatter the crumbs of his
> largesse to his exploited workers.
>   On the more positive side, labor believes that counseling

---

[4] By permission from *Employee Counseling*, Nathaniel Cantor, copyrighted, 1945,
by McGraw-Hill Book Co., Inc.

[5] Mary Palevsky, "The Union Counsels Industrial Workers," *Counseling Services
for Industrial Workers*, pages 35-42. New York: Family Service Association of
America. By permission of the publishers.

under its *own* auspices provides the workers with an opportunity for democratic self-help and self-direction . . . Because the union experiments are less well known than management-sponsored counseling, and because they have developed a special relationship to social work, we shall attempt to describe the more significant projects in brief but specific detail.

CHICAGO

The Social Service Employees Union in this city selected the United Packinghouse Workers of America as a co-sponsor for a counseling project to be used by the members of the latter union. This union was chosen because it is a progressive C.I.O. union with a membership of 25,000, of whom 25 per cent are women and 50 per cent are Negroes. The Social Service Employees Union provided the volunteer services of twelve professional social workers on a rotating basis, each volunteer contributing ten hours a month. Services were made available in the union halls once a week during evening hours. The Packinghouse Workers Union supplied the space, the telephone, clerical services, and, in addition, printed and distributed leaflets announcing the service. In bold face type, the leaflets said, "Do You Need Help? Have You a Problem? You don't have to go to Dr. Anthony. Your union has set up a special social service office at the disposal of all union members. . . ."

During the first year of operation, the workers handled 135 applications, most of which had been referred by shop stewards. Lack of housing, especially for Negroes, was a serious problem. There were many problems connected with workmen's compensation, wage garnishments, and other problems of indebtedness.

Two additional projects were subsequently made available in locals of the United Electrical, Radio, and Machine Workers, and there are demands for similar projects in other unions in Chicago.

DETROIT

The group of union social workers who established the organizing committee to sponsor a project in Detroit consisted of three representatives each of the Social Service Employees Union; the State, County, and Municipal Workers of America

(C.I.O.); and the American Federation of State, County, and Municipal Employees (A.F. of L.). The committee included two supervisors, six case workers, and one community organization worker. The Workers' Counseling Service was set up in the union halls of the United Automobile Workers of America, Local 208. This local was chosen because it is relatively small, consisting of 8,000 members. The leadership is progressive and the composition of the membership is varied. The social workers gave their services on a volunteer basis, two evenings a week and Saturdays. The usual range of family problems was presented to the counselors, with a preponderance of problems relating to taxation and legal difficulties. The union therefore engaged a tax expert to help the workers who were paying an income tax for the first time and referred the legal problems that were outside the scope of the Legal Aid Bureau to the United Automobile Workers' attorneys.

PHILADELPHIA

A similar training project for union counselors has been adopted in Philadelphia. It was initiated by the Community Relations Committee of the Philadelphia C.I.O. Industrial Union Council. The committee enlisted the help of the Council of Social Agencies and the representatives of the Regional War Production Board. The plants represented in the union counselor plan are: General Electric, Westinghouse, Electric Storage Battery Company, Cramps Shipyard, International Resistance Company, Philip E. Sheers Company, Bendix, Moore Textile Mills, and Gibbs Underwear. Social workers from the fields of child care, housing, health, and veterans' service led the classes. The first group of ten men and eleven women, selected by their unions, has completed a series of six weekly classes. Monthly clinics for consultation are planned. It is now national C.I.O. policy to encourage this plan and in a large number of cities the unions are following the example of Detroit and Philadelphia.

The family agency-union co-operative projects, described in the previous chapter as a contribution of the family agency to the welfare of war workers, might with equal logic have been included in this chapter as union-family agency projects representing a contribution of organized labor to the welfare of war workers.

LABOR AND SOCIAL WORK GET TOGETHER

The significance of these union counseling projects must be sought elsewhere than in the numbers of workers served. These have remained necessarily small in relation to the total union membership in a new service that has to feel its way cautiously around the debris of group prejudice. The projects are not deeply rooted as yet in union consciousness or usage. Not all unions are convinced that this type of welfare service is a proper function of trade unions. In the operation of an unfamiliar activity practical as well as theoretical questions arise for which there are no ready answers. Nevertheless, the social workers who are participants in these projects see in this new frontier of social work some far-reaching implications for the future of the profession.

They foresee some "retooling" of case work techniques to meet the needs of a new group of clients. While union members have the problems common to other people, they have unique ways of expressing and meeting them. When the worker seeks service from his union, he does so, not "with hat in hand," but with directness and self-confidence. Moreover, the average union member has a healthy skepticism about social work—he is from Missouri and wants to be shown in clear-cut, realistic terms what social workers can do. These considerations serve to keep social workers on their toes—an appropriate stance for a young profession.

The new union-member client is losing his fear and suspicion of social workers. . . . A social worker who is also a union brother (more often, a union sister!) seems not a bad sort when you get to know her—decent, competent, trustworthy. In learning to trust the social worker in the union, the worker is also learning to transfer his trust to the social agency. There is general agreement that the successful interpretation of the services of social agencies to large groups of workers has been an outstanding contribution of the union projects.

Union counseling provides a ready method for testing the efficacy of existing welfare services. Group problems are readily discerned and tend to highlight the gaps in community resources. One such significant problem that emerged very early, for instance, is the large number of health problems of industrial workers for which there is as yet no adequate medical coverage.

Increased contact with community agencies is stimulating the workers' interest in their programs, aims and methods. When the worker learns that he has an important stake in the social services, it is believed that he will exert himself to support and maintain high professional standards. Greater participation by workers in the programs of social agencies offers a potential contribution to the further democratization of social work and the eventual merging of the supporting constituency and the service clientele.

The fruitful collaboration of labor and social work in these union counseling projects is but one more example of the striking trend that is bringing these two movements together in the mutual recognition that they share common goals for community welfare and have need of each other for the achievement of these goals."

It is obvious that some unions have their counselors at work and are busy training additional personnel to meet the needs of their workers in matters requiring guidance and advice. The union business agent-worker relationship has always been one of a counseling nature. The fact that the term counselor has not been applied to the relationship does not lessen the similarity between the functions involved. However, the relationship that exists between the union steward and the worker when the latter's grievances are being prepared for presentation to management is one requiring counseling and guidance for the employee.

It should be quite clear at this point that if management does not furnish a counseling service and plant supervision is not such that employees turn readily to the foremen, then workers will seek out the union representative every time.[6] Whether or not this is desirable will depend upon which side of the table you are sitting as you read the statement. To the union official, the only place to turn is to the Union; to the management representative, the only place to turn is to management. A worker must make his decision as to where he will secure the assistance desired in

[6] For a further discussion of union representatives see: Leonard J. Smith, *Collective Bargaining*, pages 84-87. New York: Prentice-Hall, Inc., 1946.

settling a particular problem.   Pressure exerted by members of his working group will frequently influence an employee to choose the union steward in order to win the approval of fellow workers. Failure on the part of the counselor to satisfactorily settle a worker's problem or adjust a grievance likewise will turn an employee toward the union steward for advice.

It is the authors' opinion that there are many potential services for employees that lie outside the realm of the union steward whose function is to handle or eliminate grievances.   The plant counselor, through rendering strategic services to the employee and the employer, should prevent minor irritations from developing into serious complaints and grievances.   The counselor should complement the efforts and the work of the union steward in plants where organized labor is represented.

Questions

1. In what terms are lawyers likely to interpret labor contracts?
2. What fears do union officials express towards the counselor?
3. List several problems handled by the Chicago Union Counseling Service.
4. State some of the reasons for distrust in the union-management relationship, and indicate how you would proceed as a counselor in a situation where it is necessary to overcome the conditions you have stated.
5. Under what conditions does labor believe in counseling?
6. Cite at least three examples of paternalism.
7. How does union counseling provide a ready method for testing the efficiency of existing welfare agencies?
8. Does union counseling tend to bring labor and social workers closer together or to separate them?   Cite examples to prove your answer.
9. Where are workers likely to take their problems if management does not provide adequate counseling service?

Bibliography

Baker, Helen, *Employee Counseling*.   Industrial Relations Section, Department of Economics and Social Institutions, Princeton University, Princeton, N. J., 1944.

Clarke, Harry Newton, and Martin, E. Elmo, "Fundamentals of Business Organization, An Orientation Course. 4—Man's Place in an Organization." Chicago, Ill.: American Technical Society, 1944.

Palevsky, Mary, "Counseling Services for Industrial Workers," Family Service Association of America, 122 East 22nd St., New York 10, N. Y., 1945.

Smith, Leonard J., *Collective Bargaining*. New York: Prentice-Hall, Inc., 1946.

Related Counseling Activity   11

In ADDITION to aiding management and workers in the manner outlined in Chapters 8, 9, and 10, the counselor can be of assistance to the plant service departments. Safety and training are two fields where co-operative help and co-ordinate service yield satisfaction in terms of results obtained. Besides working with these departments, the counselor may be called upon to make known to the community the human relations and welfare activities carried on by the organization he represents. These and related activities make up a field in which the tactful counselor may profitably spend a portion of his time.

Assist with Safety Programs

Safety engineers, always on the lookout for practical suggestions, will welcome the counselor's ideas on accident prevention. Through his thorough knowledge of human reactions, the counselor should contribute greatly to improving the plant safety record.[1] He should be in a position to offer assistance in dealing with accidents that result from loss of temper, carrying a chip on one's shoulder, lack of sleep, or wool gathering.

Accidents are costing industry millions of dollars annually in decreased production; accidents are costing workers millions of dollars annually in lost wages. What is more, the worker pays in suffering as well as wages. Because of the tremendous losses involved, production specialists and safety engineers are paying increased attention to the mechanical safeguards that protect em-

---

[1] See: Joseph Tiffin, *Industrial Psychology*, pages 280-312. New York: Prentice-Hall, Inc., 1943.

ployees and insure uninterrupted output; in the matter of accident prevention counselors should devote more attention to the mental make-up of the injured individual because of the suffering and worry that are involved.   The counselor may well raise these questions: Is the employee temperamentally suited to the job? Is the proper allowance being made for fatigue?   Are there unusual working conditions such as heat, moisture, fumes, speed and other conditions that require better planning?   Is this a job for the safety engineer or a job for the human engineer?

The counselor may be able to spot an unsafe practice that is being overlooked by the employee himself: workers in unsafe positions, machines operating at dangerous speeds, and poisonous materials being handled in unventilated rooms.   Special groups including women, youths and oldsters need appropriate attention in the matter of safety.   The counselor is in a favorable position to observe and make suggestions that will prevent accidents.

Problems of nonconformity and abnormality should pass over the counselor's desk.[2]   When an individual is repeatedly involved in accidents the counselor should make the necessary investigations and recommendations.   Accident-prone individuals frequently are suffering from some extraneous exciting cause that should be removed or corrected.[3]   Included in these exciting causes are such problems as an unfaithful wife, a sick child, alimony payments, expensive payments on a new automobile or like matters that cause worry and distraction.   In these situations where the human element over-balances mechanical elements, accident prevention should be considered within the province of the counselor who is working to promote increased plant safety. Some safety engineers attribute eighty per cent of all accidents

[2] Use of the interview as a means of diagnosing worker personality and conduct is covered thoroughly by: Percival M. Symonds, *Diagnosing Personality and Conduct,* pages 450-483.   New York: Appleton-Century, Inc., 1931.

[3] The removal of some of the physical causes that make workers accident-prone will tend to build plant morale.   Personal worries also affect workers and tend to increase the accident rate and lower production.   See: "Building Morale with Medical Care," *Modern Industry,* September 15, 1946, pages 35-39.

to human difficulties rather than mechanical defects. The statement that the best safety device is an alert, careful workman emphasizes the fact that the human factors involved in safety need increased attention. The latter is the counselor's specialty, and he should continually co-operate with the safety department to reduce the accident rate.

A counselor in one large industry aided the safety department by acting as a clearing house for all safety information that appeared in various bulletins, trade journals, and safety publications. Pertinent information posted by the counselor was considered by the safety engineer to be the most valuable single contribution made to the safety program. Catchy phrases, limericks, and jingles have an appeal and we are inclined to remember best those words of caution that include a touch of humor. Who but the counselor is better prepared to determine what causes the desired reaction among employees? He is the one best able to help workers before an accident strikes. He is also well prepared to help them snap back after an accident has occurred.

Co-operate with the In-Service Training Department

There are times when the training department is not convinced of *what* training is needed *where*.[4] There are also times when the training department needs convincing evidence to submit to its superiors that training is required. The counselor can serve the training department by answering the "what and where" of training. This can be done most effectively through the use of attitude surveys. If these surveys are made by a trained and competent person, the following information may be obtained:

1. Sources of dissatisfaction
2. Nature of complaints and gripes
3. Basic causes of discontent
4. Degree of acceptance of rules, regulations and policies
5. Reactions to training and felt training needs

[4] For a discussion of training for industrial establishments read: Joseph Tiffin, *Industrial Psychology*, pages 185-216. New York: Prentice-Hall, Inc., 1943.

6. Attitude of workers toward management

7. Attitude of workers toward supervisors

8. Degree of job security felt by workers, that is, whether or not workers feel that adequate protection, compensation, insurance, pension allowances, and other security features exist

9. Proposals for providing adequate job satisfaction.

Armed with this information, the training department can plan training programs to cover all needs expressed by the workers themselves. Additional needs may be determined by polling management and the supervisory staff for their reaction to training needs.[5] Workers seem more willing to express themselves about the needs of those who are down-the-line in the wage scale than they are to speak out on the needs of employees who are higher up. Many industrial problems are the direct result of inadequate training. Poor and ineffective training comes in for its share of criticism from employees during the counseling interview. Training departments should receive this information from the counselor when planning courses for supervisors to improve worker morale.

Classify and Interpret Data on Trends

Sources of information upon which the counselor should base predictions and trends in worker demands, labor turnover, employee dissatisfaction, and the like, include departmental files and personnel reports, conference and supervisory reports, individual records and interviewing conferences, statistical data and graphic analyses. Such factual information should be subjected to a screening process that includes the following questions: What factors influence this data? What factors (over which there is seemingly no control) will continue to influence the data? What effect has personality had in the reliability of the data? These and like questions should be used to test the information gathered

[5] For information about a college training program designed to prepare students for entrance into administrative positions, and for a glimpse of the curriculum prepared for such a program of training, read: "Management Training Program, Radcliffe College, Cambridge, Mass.," *Personnel Journal*, April, 1946, pages 362-368.

before attempts are made to interpret trends. Action recommended to correct faulty supervisory practices that have been discovered should be included in any reports submitted to management.

Slow-moving general trends are sometimes overlooked. It may be as simple a matter as overloading a department with a certain type of worker. For example, too many youngsters, too many relatives, or too many elderly employees may be found in a single department instead of a balanced number of various types of employees, assuming, of course, that balance is a policy of top management.

When the statistician and the specialist in human relations join forces to point the direction in which industrial relations are moving, management usually takes note of the situation. What the general manager believes workers are thinking is not nearly so important as what the workers themselves are really thinking.[6] When a breakdown in management-employee industrial relations occurs, it is usually the result of the general manager having guessed wrong about what his workers were thinking. The alert counselor with his fingers on the pulse of the workers can give an accurate appraisal of worker demands and also worker reactions to management's proposals. These appraisals increase in value when their accuracy is later proved. Keeping up with the trends in thought among workers is an art well worth the counselor's time and effort.

Keep Necessary Records

Records kept by the counselor should not duplicate those kept elsewhere in the organization. If there is a need for records and reports that originate outside the counselor's office, copies of needed items should be requested. Confidential reports covering individuals within the plant should be properly safeguarded. Records and reports indicating the progress made by the coun-

---

[6] J. E. Eitington, "The Post-War Supervisor: Detective in Human Relations," *Personnel Journal,* May, 1947, pages 19-22.

selor should be kept readily available. This material should be prepared for management's information and guidance. The basis for such reports would be a record of all contacts made. A data sheet covering each contact made should contain the following information: name, address, age, department, date of contact, supervisor's name, problem presented by the employee, source of referral, and the action taken. Under the caption "Source of Referral" it is well to keep a record of those who suggest the counseling service as a possible answer to the problems of fellow workers. Referrals are frequently made by the personnel department, the plant nurse, the union steward, the supervisor, or the fellow at the next machine.

In classifying data for presentation to management, items of interest and of value include:

1. The number of worker-supervisor situations in which counseling played a part

2. The absenteeism and tardiness rate

3. Transfers resulting from workers' inability to make the necessary job adjustment

4. Problems involving hours, wages, and working conditions[7]

5. Educational and vocational inquiries

6. Health, personal, and financial problems, and

7. Any emotional disturbances occurring in the plant.

In many instances a résumé of the action taken should be given to indicate the type of service rendered by the counselor. Statements of interest are those that answer such questions as: How effective was the service? What was done to remedy any given situation uncovered by the counselor? Has co-operation with other departments resulted in recommendations being made to the placement, personnel, health, timekeeping, supervisory, or other departments?

---

[7] Frequently foremen are not satisfied with conditions under which they work. This fact is clearly pointed out in the following article by a foreman. It is interesting to note that supervisory counseling was given as a possible solution to the problems facing the foreman who was stating his position from a plateau of progress. "Stuck at Thirty-Five," *Personnel Journal*, January, 1946, pages 270-278.

It bears repeating here that workers do not like to be considered "cases." The counselor should not use the social worker's case-work approach or keep elaborate case records. The personal data sheet previously suggested may be prepared and kept for ready reference. If disciplinary action has been taken or a warning given, the additional information covering the results of the contact may be included in the employee's file folder in the personnel office.

Exit interviews are important as a barometer of conditions within the plant. A record should be kept of all exit interviews. Clues to the quality of supervision may be brought to light in this manner.[8] Employment practices and higher competing wage scales of other employers may be discovered early enough so that necessary adjustments can be made to retain many valuable workers. Statements made during the exit interview may prove of value in cases where employees have a change of heart after severing connections with the plant.

Make Periodic Reports to Management

Management will call upon the counselor from time to time for statements as to the degree to which human relations problems are being met by supervisors and foremen. Such reports will reveal departments that are superior in their ability to keep operations continuously at a high level while maintaining splendid worker relationships, as well as departments that need help in strengthening their worker-supervisor, worker-management, and worker-worker relationships.

Two types of reports should be made. First, a routine report taken from the regular records which are kept in the department. This should be concise and in a form which the counselor and management have agreed upon as being adequate and desirable. Each counselor should figure out techniques (according to the

---

[8] Studies of labor turnover have many practical values. The quality of supervision may be detected through turnover studies as is pointed out by: F. R. Clarke, "Labor Turnover Studies," *Personnel Journal,* June, 1946, pages 55-58.

personality and idiosyncrasies of the person to whom the report is made) of highlighting information of particular and perhaps emergent interest.   Topics should include the number of counseling interviews held, the nature of complaints and gripes, action taken to prevent recurrence of complaints, assistance offered foremen and supervisors, and routine recommendations for improvement of human relations situations within the plant.

The second type consists of "Red banner" and "Green star" reports.   The "Red banner" indicates distress or warning.   In other words, something is wrong and steps should be taken to correct the situation.   The counselor should call the attention of management to policies that need changing or to ill-administered policies—*without mentioning names or involving personalities*. "Green star" reports should be made to management on excellent procedures or policies which are paying dividends in human relations.   These reports are of special value and their use should not be overlooked.   They should include suggestions that individuals and departments receive special recognition for their efforts in bringing about a better understanding between the management and its workers.   Recognition of this kind spurs the persons concerned, as well as others, to new goals of attainment. Management's recognition of the efforts of supervisors who have an outstanding record for dealing squarely with workers will have a wholesome and far-reaching effect upon plant personnel.   Counselors may, with management's approval, prepare for signature letters or other forms of recognition to be presented as awards.[9]

Serves as a Management Representative

The alert counselor will be a member of a professional personnel organization, and may have occasion to discuss employee relations officially and unofficially while away from his business office.   Management is frequently called upon for information

---

[9] Communications from management to its workers need modernizing.   For an outstanding discussion of what is new in this field, reference should be made to the following article: "How to Tell Your Story to Workers," *Modern Industry*, May 15, 1947, pages 44-48.

about its personnel activities and its progress in the field of human relations.   The counselor may be asked to fill-in on meetings of this kind as his work increases in importance and improves in quality.

Prior to speaking at meetings that call for the discussion of plant practices and the exposition of plant policies, there should be clear-cut agreement between top management and the counselor on what information should be released.   There are certain topics which should not be discussed outside the plant "family." Similar caution should be observed when news items are released by the counselor.   He should know what these "off the record" subjects are, and should be adroit at skirting direct answers to these questions when speaking in public.   Management has a responsibility for seeing that the counselor is given all the facts concerning proposed changes in industrial relations policies.   The counselor has a responsibility for acquiring factual material that will give him an unbiased point of view on matters of interest to employees, management, and the general public.[10]   Good judgment is always involved in deciding how much information should be furnished.   The quality of any information divulged should be impeccable.   Management must assume its responsibility for furnishing the counselor with the true facts.   It may, at the same time, expect that the counselor will proceed wisely when representing management either inside or outside the plant.

Publicity may be favorable or unfavorable.   Because there is a tendency for rumors and gossip to spread rapidly throughout a plant, and because it is easier to make a point with something unfavorable than it is with something favorable, the counselor must give thought to the matter of favorable publicity.   If it is true that the best defense is a good offense, then publicity from the counseling department should be constant, favorable, and sufficient.

---

[10] For a thumbnail sketch of the manner in which a plant may be explained to the public, see: "Explaining Your Plant to the Community," *Modern Industry*, May 15, 1947, page 37.

The counselor has been cautioned against "hiding his light under a bushel" while hoping that someone will find it. Such tactics may cause unfavorable criticisms to extinguish a useful program before its value is recognized. Publicity, on the other hand, should not be of the type where its appearance has no more effect that the cry "Wolf, Wolf" by the shepherd boy.

The report to top management should be given careful consideration, and unless there is definite opposition to it, a weekly or monthly review of the counseling work should be prepared. Counseling activities are usually good for a story or two in each issue of the plant magazine. Special activities of the plant make interesting reading in the daily newspaper. Recent studies seem to indicate that most plants are seriously misunderstood in matters of wages and profits. Industry seems to have passed beyond the stage where it is willing for public opinion of plant practices and policies to be determined by the plant product alone. Possibly, in the opinion of the authors, too much publicity has already been given to some of the unfavorable practices of large corporations. The need is to get more facts to the public concerning the fairness of the employer and the wholesomeness of his employment practices.[11]

Just as the counselor must not assume that everything is fine because he has not heard anything unfavorable about his program, industry must not assume, either, that the public is fully informed and favorably impressed with all that the plant is doing. Human relations stories have great public appeal, and the wise counselor will find many of them right outside his door. Pictures and write-ups in the plant magazine may also be released in the local newspaper on the same day that the house organ is distributed to employees.

For emphasis, it is repeated here that all publicity should have

---

[11] Frequently there are too many secrets connected with the modern industrial plant. To understand how one organization overcame the problem of salary secrets read: Harvey T. Stephens, "The Story of Your Salary," *Personnel Journal*, April, 1947, pages 330-334.

the approval of management; a routine for handling matters of this kind should be worked out. In addition to newspaper releases, articles for trade journals might also be considered. Plant bulletins and well-illustrated booklets describing the services of the program make interesting reading for employees. During World War II some plants made movies that have since been given nationwide distribution. For some years the Ford Motor Company has described its policies through its weekly broadcasts. The counselor with an interest in getting the services he represents and the employer for whom he works understood will find many ways to present the facts to the public in an interesting and acceptable manner.

When the counselor is asked to speak before personnel groups, safety organizations, and luncheon clubs, still another avenue of publicity is opened to him. His conduct, appearance, mannerisms, and personality should reflect credit to the organization he represents. Speeches should be interesting and worthwhile to the audiences, since a poor showing will have the same effect as adverse publicity would have if delivered through some other media.

Questions

1. List five items to be included in a survey of the "what and where" of training.
2. What relations should the counselor have with the training section?
3. What are some of the sources of information from which the counselor may gather material upon which to base predictions and trends?
4. What records should the counselor keep?
5. What should be included in the counselor's report to management?
6. What are labeled "Red banner" and "Green star" reports?
7. How can the counselor serve management?
8. Should the counselor have speeches and talks reviewed and okayed by management? Why?
9. Name some special safety problems that the counselor may be called upon to handle.

10. If the statement, "The best possible safety device is an alert, careful workman," is true, indicate some ways in which the counselor can assist the safety engineer in improving the accident record.

Bibliography

Aspley, John Cameron, and Whitmore, Eugene, *The Handbook of Industrial Relations*.   Chicago: The Dartnell Corporation, 1945.

Beaumont, Henry, *The Psychology of Personnel*.   New York: Longmans, Green & Co., 1945.

Cooper, Alfred M., *How to Supervise People*.   New York: McGraw-Hill Book Co., Inc., 1946.

Hitchcock, C. N., *Forms, Records and Reports in Personnel Administration*.   Chicago: The University of Chicago Press, 1923.

Knowles, Asa S., and Thomson, Robert D., *Management of Manpower*.   New York: The Macmillan Co., 1943.

Tiffin, Joseph, *Industrial Psychology*.   New York: Prentice-Hall, Inc., 1943.

Good counseling begins with locating and placing in service well-qualified individuals who willingly accept responsibilities. Those who have been most successful in selecting capable counselors place emphasis upon personality. There is a tendency on the part of individuals uninitiated in the technique of counselor selection to emphasize educational qualifications to the exclusion of other factors.[1] More and more, however, we are coming to realize the greater importance of "adaptability and personal adjustment" as qualities of definite significance in the make-up of the successful counselor. There are three more basic qualifications which should be carefully investigated by employers.

1. *Objectivity*—an emotionally stable attitude. Included in this quality should be the capacity for offering sympathy without overdoing it, a genuinely receptive and interested attitude, and deep understanding which will make it impossible for the counselor to be prejudiced or be easily shocked or horrified—in other words, a condition of controlled composure.

2. *Respect for the individual.* There must be a strong desire and a ready willingness to treat all workers as individuals. The counselor must gather not only facts but also the thoughts and opinions of his counselees; the person who would succeed in counseling must treat each employee with appropriate consideration.

3. *Self-understanding.* Unless the counselor is aware of his

---

[1] War Manpower Commission, *The Training of Vocational Counselors*, pages 5-39. Washington, D. C.: Superintendent of Documents, Government Printing Office, 1944.

own limitations and short-comings and tries to remedy them, he will not be likely to succeed in the counseling position.

Personal Traits and Their Relationship to Counseling

Personal traits that go to make up an integrated, well-balanced personality are prime requisites for success in the counseling field. Regardless of the specific counseling assignment, be it in government service, school activity, or industrial management, personality is the element with carry-over value.

The counselors being sought by employers today possess in great abundance traits that are identified in the discussion that follows. Good counselors need these resources. They are definite aids in solving the problems of personnel adjustment and job efficiency.

Mature Judgment

Frequently, persons who are seeking counsel are willing and ready to clutch at straws. Regardless of the quality of the counselor's suggestions the latter will be accepted or tried. It is of vital importance, therefore, that the counselor possess sufficiently mature judgment to distinguish readily between right and wrong.

In the problem solving phase of the counselor's work, logical reasoning is helpful in getting necessary facts.[2] From the volume of material poured out by the counselee, the alert counselor must arrange the information logically to identify the problem. Good common sense (here the authors wish to imply a keen sense of timing) woven into workable suggestions goes a long way toward getting the job done.

Using mature judgment, logical reasoning, and good common sense to gather, organize, catalogue, and disseminate helpful information can make the counselor the focal point of service for

---

[2] Personnel research utilized to get the facts and to draw honest conclusions from the facts is discussed by B. W. Elsom, Superintendent of Personnel and Service, Milwaukee Boston Store, Milwaukee, Wisconsin, in an article entitled "Personnel Research," *Personnel Service,* November-December, 1945, pages 28-31.

those persons who are striving to adjust themselves. Unfortunately, however, the personality, intelligence, and aptitude tests now available do not measure adequately the judgment, reasoning, and common sense capacities of counselors.   The hiring interview may reveal bold weaknesses in reasoning or judgment, but this initial interview may not find the candidate capable of consistently making wise decisions.   A review of the counselor's previous employment experiences may furnish the management with some clues as to how well the prospective counselor made decisions involving reasoning and good common sense.   Emotional instability, warped personality, or other outward evidences of eccentricity hardly give promise of success in the counseling field.

Ability to Listen

Objectivity is extremely desirable when getting the facts. Mental and physical composure give wider opportunity to interpret implied meanings beyond the words uttered by the counselee, who may be neither calm nor coherent.[3]   An alert listening attitude is probably one of our most severe concentration tests.   A counselor who goes woolgathering while listening may find his success short-lived.   Equally brief is the success of the hot-tempered individual who cannot listen to details without interrupting or exploding.   The interviewee will probably become non-committal if he feels that a reprimand or a blow-up is in the offing.

The counselor must keep under his hat much of the information that counselees give him.   Keeping one's own counsel should include absorbing much information, transmitting it into possible action, and locking up the details upon which the action is based. There should be no room in the counselor's program for broadcasting information that will put the counselee "on the spot" with management or result in his being "told off" by fellow workers. Information which does not *help* the counselee is best forgotten.

------

[3] The demand for specific information by counselees is making the work of the counselor increasingly challenging.   Paul T. Kosiak, "Common-sense Counseling," *Personnel Journal,* April, 1947, pages 343-352.

Resourcefulness and Reliability

Few of us would score one hundred per cent if rated accurately on these qualities, but an honest estimate can be placed upon the prospective counselor's possession of them. Scores should be determined in the light of the following considerations:

1. The kind and amount of freedom of action allowed the counselor
2. The nature of the problems to be dealt with by the counselor
3. The degree of control exercised by the superior to whom the counselor is responsible
4. The general composition of the counselee group
5. The size of the organization in which the counselor works.

Generally speaking, new ideas are readily accepted by the open-minded, co-operative person. The counselor should be quick to put into practice those changes that management suggests. The honest, reliable person will be dependable in the performance of duties in accordance with daily requirements.

In some discussions of counseling, the ideal counselor is pictured as a sort of psychological superman—all wise, all knowing, and omniactive. This is far from realistic thinking, because no one person can be *all things* at *all times*. Possession of an open mind to receive information and the ability to refrain from passing on of facts and opinions requires no super-human qualities, but it does call for constant exercise in mental discipline.

A co-operative spirit is fundamental to success in all supervisory or management positions; many of the desirable qualities of a good counselor are equally important to the manager and supervisor. If the foreman and the supervisor are to handle human relations problems as intelligently as the counselor, training must be provided that will put these key individuals on an equal footing with labor leaders.[4] Many of the other qualities we will review are of equal value to counselor, supervisor, and manager alike.

---

[4] This point is developed rather fully in a well illustrated article: "Tying Supervision Into Management," *Modern Industry*, October 15, 1946, pages 38-42.

A Counselor's Vocabulary

On-the-job experience is the best means for increasing and improving the counselor's understanding of counselees' problems. It is reasonable to assume that the counselor who has never been employed in a factory may neither speak nor have the ability to understand the language of an industrial worker. Likewise, one who has never worked in government service may find it difficult to counsel government workers satisfactorily. Similarly, a person who had not attended college would find counseling on this level "beyond his depth."

Some industries, sensing the limitations of counselor training and its application to the job, have seen fit to provide a period of on-the-job experiences for prospective counselors. This arrangement gives the counselor insight into certain problems, and a point of view oriented to the specific plant and employee group.[5] While working shoulder to shoulder with plant employees, the counselor can pick up the "lingo" of the plant and obtain an over-all view of the plant production system.

A Sense of Humor

Perhaps a person can do a good counseling job without possessing a sense of humor, but having a sense of humor will make it easier to meet many difficult situations. Helping others to see the amusing side of little problems frequently staves off the unpleasantness associated with larger problems. Timing is one consideration of paramount importance in the use of humor. Workers should not be made the butt of a joke, nor offended by either deliberate or thoughtless sarcasm.

One of the best uses of humor results from the counselor's pointing out the lighter side of some problem or set of circumstances which surround a worker's problem. The goal is the

---

[5] To gain some understanding of what goes on in the worker's mind, a rather careful reading of the following article is suggested: Edward J. Redmon, "The Factory Mind," *Personnel Journal*, June, 1946, pages 59-61.

transforming of a mountain into a molehill through bringing the facts into proper perspective. Most situations have some points which are on the "right," good, or positive side of the ledger. A resourceful counselor capitalizing on these facts can lift morale with a pleasing smile and an explanation of the redeeming factors.

Humor does not fit into every situation, but it will be of value in proving that the counselor can "take it" as well as give it. Because a worker gets hot-headed, the counselor need not follow suit. The latter's genuine amiability may be the factor which tips the scales in his favor in solving the problem.

Constructive Criticism

Management and employees will not always select the proper time or place to offer criticism of the counselor's work. The counselor, therefore, must make allowances for disturbing comments and gracefully accept criticism even if it is not skillfully or tactfully given. His own resentment and retaliation must be overcome quickly if the counseling job is to be done successfully.

Because the counselor is the "friendly listening post of the plant," he should possess the faculty for receiving all kinds of criticism in the best father-confessor manner. Holding one's temper and getting the whole story is not an easy assignment; yet, to interrupt, censure, or retaliate defeats the objective of good counseling.

It should be emphasized that in counseling the mere *giving* of constructive criticism does not necessarily remedy the situation. Constructive criticism should inspire the receiver to correct the errors that have occurred. Much preventive work can be accomplished with properly timed suggestions that preclude serious breaks within an organization. Where criticism is given, it should be weighed in advance for its constructive qualities.

Unless the worker has been aroused to the point of *wanting* to use the help given, any advice, no matter how desirable, is just words. Follow-up, therefore, is important when giving constructive suggestions. One might tell the counselee, "Let me know how this works. I am going to check back with you in a few days to see how you have worked this problem out."

Personal Integrity

Personal integrity is a quality acquired through education, association, and co-operation.   It involves an attitude towards right living and right acting.   The person who rates highest in personal integrity usually possesses mental poise, emotional stability, and just convictions.   Honesty, fairness, impartiality and an adherence to the rules of the game make favorable impressions upon workers.   These qualities are essential to the counselor who, more than any other one person, is responsible for keeping employee morale at a high level.

Promises made or implied by the counselor must be fulfilled, or the worker should be told why keeping the promise was impossible.   The counselor will do well to make few promises and to keep those he makes.   When workers feel that their superiors are unfair, forgetful, inconsiderate, or incompetent, the tendency to run down the management grows.[6] From a labor supply point of view, and during periods of normal labor market activity, this may or may not be a hardship on an organization, but during World War II the War Manpower Commission found it difficult to recruit workers for industries where lack of confidence in management integrity was well known.   When worker morale is considered, there is a need for management representatives to be fair at *all* times.

Individuals known for their personal integrity have developed the habit of considering the other fellow's point of view.   If under such a test the action to be taken does not ring true, sound fair, or measure up, another course of action must be planned. The wise counselor will know the chronic gripers in the plant and will weight his recommendations accordingly.   Being honest and fair-minded does not mean that biased or easy-going deci-

---

[6] Robert D. Loken, "Warm or Cold Management?" *Personnel Journal*, February, 1946, pages 308-317.

sions should be made in an attempt to please certain employees.

The counselor's personal adverse opinion of supervisors and managers must not reach the work-force. Personal integrity in the counselor alone is not enough. Every supervisor and every manager should merit the respect of most employees if morale is to be sufficiently high to radiate a feeling that the organization is united in its effort to reach a wholly desirable, unified goal.

The wise counselor will unite the supervisory force in an effort to maintain practices that build loyalty in the minds and hearts of the workers. Look deeply into any plant where every worker is a booster and you will find that personnel practices reflect fair-mindedness, honesty, tolerance, and integrity.[7] These qualities can be developed only if top management fosters and promotes them.

Practical Experience for Veterans' Counselors

Counselors of veterans have been brought into service from many fields and a great wealth of material has been prepared on how to do this specialized counseling. Because many veterans' counselors lack actual experience in adult counseling techniques, it is likely that dissatisfaction will be expressed concerning ineptness in handling veterans' cases.[8]

This weakness indicates that there is a missing step between the printed instructions of the Veterans Administration or the Employment Service and the actual counseling job. There should be introduced an "application step," under the tutelage of a skillful counselor, where new workers in the veterans' counseling field learn to apply the principles of good counseling and

---

[7] Removing the source of trouble rather than just hushing it up gives workers a sense of fair dealing. Thompson Products, Inc., has a program to cure grievances: "Stopping Grievances Before They Grow," *Modern Industry*, February 15, 1947, pages 49-64.

[8] The treatment of veterans in industry opens a new field of activity for personnel workers. Two fundamental principles seem to obtain: (1) forget the war, and (2) do not molly-coddle. For a complete discussion of this line of reasoning see: George E. Tucker, "Veterans in Industry," *Personnel Journal*, March, 1946, pages 334-337.

also to interpret the directives and policies of the Veterans Administration, Employment Service, or other agencies.   Practical experience for the veterans' counselor should include a period of internship in the modern techniques of counseling.   Veteran counselors should also have a background of first-hand experience in dealing with administrators in business, industry, government, and education.   Previous employment in contact work, selling, or business administration should prove helpful to the counselor.

Skill in interviewing must be developed if it is not already a part of the counselor's experience.   Knowledge of the various fields of occupational opportunity is obviously an essential.   A broad understanding of the philosophies of various job-training programs is vital to vocational counselors.   For example, a counselor who does not understand bona fide apprenticeship may recommend against it due to personal prejudices.   When information concerning the counselor's action reaches the apprentice-training services the real facts are likely to be distorted sufficiently to make a real bogey-man out of the counselor.   In summary, the greater the breadth of any counselor's practical experience in previous jobs, the more wisely can he perform his task.

The Industrial Counselor's Work Experience

The industrial counselor has a great responsibility in keeping operations moving forward smoothly; it is important therefore, that these counselors should have had work experience that has made them thoroughly familiar with:

1. Industrial plant procedures involved in:
    a. Meeting production schedules
    b. Operating at a profit
    c. Establishing lines of authority
    d. Staff, line, and functional organization
2. The importance of co-ordination and co-operation
3. The duties and responsibilities of supervisory personnel.

Experience which has provided for understanding people and the worker's relationship to his job would be most valuable.   The counselor should recognize occupational trends and be able to interpret labor market information. Experience in the application of labor relations and counseling techniques (see pages 100-103) and the desire to keep abreast of significant industrial changes are prerequisites in the make-up of an industrial counselor. As has been mentioned earlier, a short workout in the plant to become acquainted with the men and women and production processes will do much towards giving an otherwise well-qualified person the "feel" of the organization.

Certain types of previous experience indicate, in a broad way, individuals who are not likely to succeed in counseling. Lawyers are apt to be too technical in their exact adherence to, and interpretation of, rules and regulations.

The teacher may carry some of the classroom techniques into counseling. Lectures are not popular with workers any more than they are with students. Regardless of worthwhile past experiences, individuals with a special pipeline to the big boss will find the going tough.[9] Acquaintance or relationship with the president, the board of directors, or the manager is not sufficient in itself to qualify one for a counseling position. When the news leaks out, and it will in spite of the remoteness of the kinship, worker morale may be adversely affected.

Counselors may be recruited from many fields, and no rules can be laid down where one will or will not find a good counselor. A person who has had some supervisory experience, knows lines of authority, likes people, and understands the local plant, should be considered if he has had the work experience necessary to do the job.

The Counselor's Educational Background

The college graduate is usually preferred because much of the counselor's time must be spent in acquiring, interpreting, and disseminating information. Reporting and a minimum of record-keeping are also considered to be necessary counselor tasks. The

---

[9] "Maker of Managers," *Modern Industry,* June 15, 1946, pages 67-78.

person with a good educational background is usually equipped to do a more comprehensive job that is satisfactory to both management and its employees. A college degree can be an asset, but the degree does not necessarily guarantee success for the counselor. It can be a real handicap if the possessor feels so superior that he acts aloof. Prospective counselors who possess the other requirements already defined should become adjusted quickly to the counseling job even though they are not college graduates.

College-trained people seem quite indispensable in school counseling. In other fields of activity, however, specialized evening school courses make possible the completion of educational requirements and advanced training which will improve the counselor's job performance.

Other Significant Considerations

Age and Health

Education and work experience are acquired and a well-balanced personality developed over varying periods of time. It would be rare, indeed, to find a well-qualified counselor who is in his early twenties. A counselor must have unlimited energy, enthusiasm, and alertness. Good physical and mental health tend to radiate a "lift" to those who come in contact with the buoyant counselor.

Duties to Be Performed

Counseling jobs vary. A management job analysis should furnish a description of the job to be done. Qualifications should be set up and evaluated in terms of the duties to be performed. The ability to get along well with plant employees, supervisors, and managers must always be considered in the selection of a person to function as counselor. Other services required by the management will dictate what additional basic qualifications the prospective counselor should possess. If management wants a splendid recreational program in addition to high plant morale, the qualifications of one person might declare that he be chosen; if management felt the need for improvement in statistical data covering what its employees are thinking, another person might be selected.   Management must determine the scope of the counseling job to be done before it settles upon the qualifications of its counselor.   The main duties (see pages 184-186) deemed desirable should set the pace for the counselor's qualifications.   The fewer the number of functions to be performed the more readily a candidate will be found to fill the vacancy.

Appearance and Manner

If the counselor is to represent management outside the establishment, it would be well to consider personal appearance, manner, and conversational ability.   On certain occasions it is even more important to know *what not to say* than to have the ability to "express one's self well." [10]   To be discreet in both speech and action is of great value to the counselor who represents management.

Job Interest

A sincere interest in counseling and the desire to do an outstanding job should not be overlooked.   If an individual is working only for payday or secretly wishes to be doing something else, the usual difficulties of handling the day-to-day problems are increased.   Dr. Carl R. Rogers makes the following statement regarding qualifications:

> Perhaps the first qualification for a counselor is that he should be a person who is sensitive to human relationships. This is a quality which is difficult to define satisfactorily but which is evident in almost any social situation.   The person who is quite obtuse to the reactions of others . . . who does not sense the hostility or friendliness which exists between him-

---

[10] Taking the wind out of public relations talk is an important service to industry these days.   This subject is dealt with in down-to-earth fashion by the editor of *Modern Industry* in an article entitled "Why Public Relations?" October 15, 1946, page 188.

self and others or between two of his acquaintances, is not likely to become a satisfactory counselor.[11]

Types to Avoid

The "Nosey" Person

When the counselor gets more satisfaction out of hearing the details than in doing something about them, effective counseling is not a likely outcome. A desire to run things that knows no bounds is apt to bring personal drives, urges, and frustration to bear upon the subject at hand. Signs of a "nosey" attitude or a display of unwarranted authority on the part of the counselor will seriously disrupt the human relationships in any organization and should not be tolerated by management. The motherly type assumes too much responsibility for the lives of others. Trying to direct the counselee beyond his wishes usually results in an aloof attitude on the part of the counselee.

The Pedant

Teaching experience can be a valuable asset to the counselor if such characteristics as the ability to express one's self well, the ability to get along well with people, the ability to lead groups, and similar items are carried over in a reasonable degree to the counseling field. There is the danger, however, of applying the whole gamut of teaching techniques to the counselor's job and paying too much attention to very small details. Frequently, the unsuccessful teacher and the unsuccessful counselor alike try to create an "aura of importance" for matters of tremendous insignificance.

The "Clinging Vine"

If a counselor does not stand on his own feet, he must accept the eventual decision of dismissal. The Milquetoast type of man

---

[11] Carl R. Rogers, *Counseling and Psychotherapy,* page 254. Boston: Houghton Mifflin Company, 1942.

and clinging-vine type of woman cannot hope to be successful counselors. The counselor's bearing, personality, and strength of character will be measured by the confidence that he instills in the minds of those who use his services. Undesirable habits and personality traits cannot be changed overnight, but with constant effort they can be modified or improved. To be successful in helping others counselors must first understand themselves, have confidence in themselves, their job, and the management; second, have no offensive mannerisms; and, third, strive to be honest, helpful and sincere. Failure to stand up for one's convictions when one is right may be as wrong as to fight for something known to be erroneous.

The Uplifter

A desire to reform the world, however noble, is not a task for the counselor. Counselees must be accepted as they are, without a word of condemnation. We cannot fit the lives of others into the pattern we have accepted as being our own goal of attainment. There are various levels of adjustment and social acceptance as well as there are varying degrees of goodness. Not everyone may wish to attain or accept our standards.

One of the gravest mistakes a counselor can make is to assume that he has a God-given mission to reform and correct all the errors he sees. Counseling is not a reforming process any more than it is a process whereby a worker tells his troubles and someone prescribes a cure-all.

Desirable Personality and Ability Traits for Counselors

1. Ability to gain and keep the trust of workers
2. Ability to inspire confidence and better work performance in workers
3. Ability to understand human nature
4. Ability to put one's self in another person's place
5. Ability to be a good listener
6. Ability to be sympathetic, but not soft

7. Above average in sincerity and loyalty
8. Above average in initiative and resourcefulness
9. Above average intelligence
10. Above average in flexibility—adaptable to many types of people and problems
11. A friendly attitude and a genuine interest in people
12. Possess a sense of humor
13. Possess good judgment and integrity
14. A sense of purpose and direction
15. Organizational ability
16. Patience
17. A co-operative attitude
18. Trustworthiness
19. Open-mindedness.

Other significant qualities of the good counselor include:

1. Ability to recognize the significance of the worker's problems
2. Ability to accept and work with people whose attitudes reflect varied nationality, economic, and social backgrounds
3. Capacity to encourage the interviewee to discuss his problem and formulate his own plans for solution
4. Ability to close an interview or a series of interviews without alienating interviewees
5. Ability to use information from records, reports, and interviews to best possible advantage
6. Desire to be a good counselor and a sincere interest in serving management and all its employees
7. Enthusiasm for self-improvement and professional development.[12]
8. A keen social sensitivity in human relationships. To paraphrase Carl Rogers, quoted on page 174, the person who is not

---

[12] The requirements of tomorrow's counselor may be drawn in more exacting terms than were the qualifications of those who held counselor jobs during World War II. What will the counselor of tomorrow have by way of background? One answer to this question is given by: H. W. Wedaa, "Tomorrow's Counselor," *Personnel Journal,* April, 1945, pages 392-396.

aware of the reactions manifested by others, who does not realize the effect of his words on the peace of mind of fellow beings, or who does not have the faculty of detecting the difference between animosity and an amicable attitude which exists between himself and others, is not likely to become a good counselor. This characteristic can be developed, but unless one has a considerable degree of this social sensitivity, it is doubtful that counseling is his most promising field of effort.

Where Management May Locate a Qualified Person

WITHIN THE ORGANIZATION

1. Study the records and personnel jackets or folders of employees, and consider supervisors who have demonstrated ability and leadership and who have a well-balanced personality.

2. Observe employees at work.

3. Get co-operation of Department Heads to assist in selecting employees who have demonstrated ability and promise.

4. Circularize the job opening. Note: There are dangers involved in circularization, as it may lower the morale of an employee who applies for the job and is not selected.

5. Study applications of those seeking jobs. Only in rare instances will ordinary applicants be found to possess the qualifications of a counselor.

OUTSIDE AGENCIES

1. Vocational training schools
2. Colleges
3. Veterans' Placement Officer —Public Employment Office
4. United States Civil Service
5. State Employment Services
6. Literature of the Counseling Field

Tests as an Aid in Selection

Personality tests can be used as an aid in the selection of a counselor. It should be clearly understood, however, that tests should be used only by people who are skilled in using them and in interpreting the scores. It is better not to use them at all unless a fully qualified person can administer and interpret them. The training department in larger plants or the Public Employment Service should be helpful in this regard. Tests serve the useful purpose of weeding out those least likely to succeed in counseling, yet even this evidence is not always one hundred per cent foolproof.

Of necessity these tests are very general in nature and are not adapted to any particular field of activity. Individuals taking these tests will not be able to see the relationship between the questions asked in the tests and their particular job. However, the essential personality traits (see pages 176-178) will show up even though the questions bear no relation to the job. Some companies have employed test experts to adapt test questions to the particular job involved. One advantage in the procedure is that the employee or applicant sees no connection between the test and his job. The following personality tests are suggested:

1. The Adjustment Inventory—Adult Form, by Hugh M. Bell, Stanford University Press, California

2. Test of Practical Judgment by A. J. Cardell, Science Research Associates, 1700 Prairie Avenue, Chicago, Illinois

3. The Personality Inventory, by Robert G. Bernreuter, Stanford University Press, Stanford University, California

4. Judgments and Characteristics of Socially Competent Persons by Mort, Spence, Arnspiger and Eads; Bureau of Publications, Teachers College, Columbia University, New York City.

The last mentioned test is excellent but was worded for High School Students. It is suggested that this factor be explained before using it.

Summary

Management's job of selecting a counselor is a difficult one. An interview cannot possibly bring out a person's true qualifications. It is necessary to know a person well or be able to obtain a true history, biographical sketch, and opinions of others before determining, for instance, whether he is co-operative or resourceful; tests are not conclusive proof. The basic factors to keep in mind are: (1) duties the counselor will be expected to perform; (2) enthusiastic attitude; (3) background of appropriate experience and training.

Questions

1. When selecting a counselor, what is the value of personal traits?
2. Why are mature judgment, logical reasoning, and common sense valuable traits for a counselor?
3. Why should a counselor be able to listen well, and keep an even temperament?
4. How can the employer determine the degree of resourcefulness, tolerance, openmindedness, etc., needed by a counselor?
5. Why does the counselor need work experience comparable to the work performed in the plant?
6. How can criticisms be made effectively?
7. What is personal integrity? Discuss its value.
8. What educational background is needed by the counselor?
9. List 15 desirable personality traits and abilities to be considered in selecting a counselor.
10. What considerations should an employer take into account when hiring a counselor?

Bibliography

Baker, Helen, *Employee Counseling*, Industrial Relations Section, Department of Economics and Social Institutions. Princeton University, Princeton, N. J., 1944.

Newman, Dorothy K., "The Woman Counselor in War Industries—An Effective System," U. S. Department of Labor, Special Bulletin No. 16. Washington: Superintendent of Documents, Government Printing Office, 1944.

"The Employee Counselor in Industry." Policyholders Service Bureau, Metropolitan Life Insurance Company, New York.

THE plant foreman in a complex industrial setup deals with men, tools, materials, machines and production.   But too often, human relations and behavior are not fully understood nor comprehensively studied by those in supervisory positions.   The counselor, on the other hand may know little about the inanimate tools of production; his specialty is human relations and human behavior.   His skill in these fields permits him to maintain a wholesome working relationship with each member of the organization, from the highest ranking person down to the prospective employee who does not yet have his foot on the bottom rung of the employment ladder.   Success for the counselor is measured in terms of how well he assists all members in their relationships with fellow workers.

Selecting a Staff

The qualifications of a good counselor were described in Chapter 12, and it is hoped that top management or the personnel director will have selected a person competent to conduct a program of counseling.   If a well qualified individual has been chosen, the counseling program is off to a good start.   Testing techniques should be employed by the personnel manager to determine latent talents of the counselor or submerged obstacles that were not in evidence during the hiring interview.   If the plant does not have a testing program, the services of a recognized psychologist might be utilized.

When new members are added to the counseling staff, it is important to consider the opinions of incumbent counselors. If effective counseling service is to be provided in a large organization, interviewing, stenographic, testing, and other assistants may be added, all of whom will require immediate supervisory and administrative leadership.

Job descriptions and job analyses should be prepared as the number of positions in the counseling department increases.[1] A control chart which permits the visualization of all jobs and the names of persons occupying them may be required by the chief counselor. Such a chart will be a great help in keeping each member informed of his position in the plant organizational structure. The chief counselor and the personnel director may find it helpful to prepare a master chart of all departments under their supervision.

It is recommended that a counselor be selected, tried, and proved before any staff increases are made. The counselor who has demonstrated the necessary leadership qualities should be given recommendatory power in the selection of additional staff members and co-workers. Responsibilities for other phases of the counseling program may be assigned by top management to a chief counselor as the latter demonstrates his ability. Some personnel directors will be reluctant to relinquish supervisory, managerial, or administrative responsibility to the person detailed to function as head or chief counselor. Whether or not authority to carry out a particular function is delegated will usually depend, however, upon the demonstrated capability of the chief counselor and the number of responsibilities confronting the personnel director.

Duties and Responsibilities Defined

Many of the duties and responsibilities of the counselor are the complex off-shoots of other service problems. As production

---

[1] Greater use of the tools developed by the Public Employment Service is part of the program of progressive counseling and personnel work. William O. Nichols, "A New Tool for Counseling," *Occupations*, Journal of the National Vocational Guidance Association, Inc., New York, May, 1945, pages 447-450.

problems have increased, foremen have found less and less time for dealing with the human relations problems of employees; as personnel departments have absorbed more and more of the responsibility, certain functions have had to be specialized and centralized. Persuasive efforts of unions to get action on matters that formerly were permitted to drift have focused attention on the social and economic needs of workers. The search for someone who could cope capably with many of the knotty problems involved has resulted in our present counseling programs.

The counseling service has assisted top and middle management with many human and industrial relations responsibilities because it has been found that many difficulties start out in the production room. Such problems can best be settled by someone who possesses the qualifications outlined in Chapter 12, and who is familiar with conditions in the plant.

During the past ten years activities of the personnel department have increased. Safety measures, social security, group savings, and many other personnel services have been inaugurated and developed. Recreation, for example, has become "big time" with bowling leagues, ball teams, glee clubs, study groups, and a generous sprinkling of other diversions. All recreational activity must be publicized, organized and supervised. To understand fully the growth of recreational activities in an industrial plant is to understand one phase of the scope and complexity of the personnel director's job. He, above all others, has sensed keenly the need of assistance from a specialist in human relations problems.

It is well recognized that our society has become increasingly complex while acquiring seemingly greater security.[2] Social agencies and regulatory bodies have grown in number and in size. An agency exists to meet nearly every given set of social maladjustments. Few there are, however, who can name the specific agency or the person in the agency to be contacted when trying to meet a given situation. Untangling these complicated, interlaced

---

[2] Boris M. Stanfield, "Our Class Struggle," *Personnel Journal*, September, 1945, pages 96-100.

social strands—bureaus, divisions, departments, administrations, corporations, and agencies—is just one more responsibility for the counselor.

For some time management has felt pressure from foremen, personnel directors, and the workers themselves for someone who would sympathetically assist employees in solving their problems. In many instances, the counselor has been brought into the plant for just this purpose. The duties of the counselor have been defined by many individuals. It should be patent that a counselor cannot be all things to all people at all times, although a composite of these definitions leads one to believe that some counselors have tried to be all things to all people.

Duties of the counselor are many and varied, depending largely upon the objectives of the program. Here is a fairly inclusive list of counselor duties.

1. Develop and maintain a courteous and reliable informational service adequate for the workers' and management's needs in the following fields:

Wage payment plans[3]   Loans and Credit Unions
Efficiency or merit ratings   Dissemination of plant infor-
Payroll deductions   mation (notices, bulletins,
Legal services   etc.)
Community welfare facilities   Medical care
Recreation   Transportation

2. Assist supervisors with human relations problems:

Inducting and orienting workers
Interpreting plant policies, rules, regulations, and practices for
    workers
Eliminating worker irritations
Following-up on new workers
Explaining pay shortages
Getting individuals to work together harmoniously

[3] Joseph H. Frost, "Personnel Paradoxes," *Personnel Journal,* March, 1946, pages 329-333.

Advising supervisors on matters of policy or regulation
Assisting with disciplinary problems
Recommending changes in working conditions
Helping with personal problems of workers
Assisting with job adjustment problems
Handling transfers
Handling requests for leaves of absence
Enforcing regulations
Assisting supervisors to overcome personal weaknesses

3. Assist the personnel director in special assignments:

Preparing employees' handbooks
Conducting interviews
Conducting supervisory conferences
Determining employee needs for improved physical facilities
Contacting community agencies
Reporting welfare or other needs to community agencies
Initiating community programs to meet workers' needs[4]
Determining "job attitudes" and making suggestions for improvement where needed
Investigating recommended discharges
Discovering potential supervisory material

4. Provide workers with an efficient service that handles the following items:

Medical appointments	Messenger service
Dental appointments	Extension of credit
Legal services	Home nursing
Budgeting programs	Community resources
Child care	Community contacts
Housing problems	Training facilities
Postal service	Health programs

---

[4] Community relations are becoming increasingly important to industrial plants. With the end of the war and the end of the rapid influx of workers to sparsely settled areas, community services are less heavily taxed than before. The problem today may be one of making the community aware of the importance of the plant to the lives of its citizens. For a discussion of this topic see: "Gaining Friends for Your Plant," *Modern Industry*, January 15, 1947, pages 34-39.

5. Offer a high-type consulting service to all plant personnel:

Suggesting solutions to personal problems
Conferring with executives on personnel problems
Discussing proper personal conduct with workers and foremen
Assisting in the solution of financial problems
Providing a place to "blow off steam," expose gripes, and make
    complaints

Introducing the Counseling Program

In a small organization members of the supervisory staff should be contacted individually. If there is a large supervisory group or if a comprehensive counseling service is being inaugurated, a special introduction meeting is desirable. The objectives of the newly adopted counseling program should be explained and the functions of the counseling staff should be made clear at this meeting. Many plants have found it advantageous to provide a discussion and questioning period for supervisors so that they will understand the purpose and the scope of the undertaking. Workers, too, should know what the counseling program can do for them; some plants arrange for frequent meetings at which new counselors are introduced and the counseling program explained. The mere posting of notices announcing the inauguration of the program is neither wise nor effective. Counseling is essentially a human relations matter and should not be mechanized or routinized. The program needs sincerity, consideration for the individual, and a person-to-person attitude; without these characteristics it is doomed to failure before it starts. Therefore, personal introductions of the counselor and his program to all plant personnel are highly desirable.

Providing Space for the Counselor

The counselor does not need elaborate quarters from which to conduct an effective program.[5] When considering the amount of space needed by the counselor, thought should be given to two

[5] Dorothy Rossback, "Modernized Personnel Offices," *Personnel Service*, March-April, 1946, page 20.

phases of the program.   The first takes place near the personnel director's headquarters where a central counseling office should provide a minimum of sixty square feet of space per staff member. Private, soundproofed offices should be available for interviewing. Provision must be made for files, bulletin boards, office equipment and the like.   The space requirements of a single counselor may be no greater than those of a stenographer.   However, counseling is a management function, and a poor looking setup is apt to produce undesirable results.

Interviewing is a process that should not be hurried nor interrupted.   Privacy for counseling interviews is an absolute necessity.   The location selected for the counseling office should provide maximum quiet and a minimum of interruptions.   The physical setup provided the counselor will have direct bearing upon the effectiveness of the program.   Adequate space is of greater importance than elaborate arrangements and equipment; the office space provided should be a model of good lighting, ventilation, and color harmony, and its comfort and convenience should set an example of good taste to those who seek help.   Clerical assistants who are quiet, capable, and efficient will, of course, add to the counselor's effectiveness.

The program's second phase takes place out in the plant near the production line.   If the plant is large, counselor quarters on the production floor should be located near the canteen, smoking room, or similar recreational facilities.   A location of this kind makes possible casual appearing trips that do not arouse employee curiosity or suspicion.   A space six feet square would do the job, but, again, management must not lose sight of the fact that employees are likely to estimate the value management places on the program by the physical setup it provides for the counselor. Every effort should be made to provide reasonable space in the production room for the counselor.   This space should not be considered to be an office nor a hangout; it is a private counseling room to be used only for business purposes.   If it is expected that women are to use the counseling room, it should be located away from the men's showers, lockers, or toilet rooms.   A glass enclosed office that spotlights the counselees will reduce the effectiveness of the interview.   Above all, the counselor and the foreman must not be expected to share the same space.

Equipment

Each interviewing room should provide comfortable chairs for the counselor and the counselee.   It is expected that the counselor will have a desk or table suited to the responsibilities of his job.   Stenographic help should be provided with adequate and comfortable office equipment.   In addition to standard letter files, several card files will be found useful.   Reference reading material will be one item that management may find it difficult to provide.   So much of what is available is scattered throughout the literature of the personnel field that a library of many volumes is needed to get the whole story.   The purchase of tests and testing equipment may be a second item which the counselor may have to justify.[6]   However, the use of carefully selected test batteries such as those suggested on pages 178-179 enables the counselor to discover hidden abilities and drives of workers, information that is useful in determining solutions to problems. The counselor may need considerable coaching and training before he is qualified to carry on an adequate testing program, but to begin slowly and continue to make progress will bring about stability in the work force through better selection of employees for each job.   If the supervision of the recreational activities of the plant is assigned to the counselor, the question of how much equipment to purchase must be answered.   A budget should, of course, be set up to determine expenses.   Band, bowling, and boxing equipment (to mention a few activities at the beginning of the alphabet) cost money, but management is usually liberal with recreational funds that yield proportionate results in worker satisfaction.

[6] For a discussion of the tests that aid in guidance and placement work consult: Frederick N. Brokaw, "The Use of Aptitude and Performance Tests in Placement Work," *Proceedings,* Twenty-eighth Annual Convention, International Association of Public Employment Services, 1940, pages 51-53.

Types of Services

The industrial counselor serves three distinct groups: top management, middle management, and plant employees. Because personal and job problems affect production, it has been found helpful to assist employees in arriving quickly at satisfactory solutions. The main effort of the industrial counselor should be focused upon problem solving.

"Problem solving" is a term which may be used to sum up the activities of a plant counselor. Employees often present problems which involve housing, transportation, recreation, safety, health, wages, hours, leave, child care, household management, and matrimony.[7] These do not exhaust the possible items, for the list is being added to almost daily in industrial establishments. Some problems which will challenge the counselor of tomorrow have not yet arisen.

Employees need someone who will listen while they "let down their hair" or "blow off steam," and who will assist them in clearing up their thinking. A counselor should not be surprised occasionally to find that even the "big boss" requests help. However, there will be many occasions when it will be necessary to probe and "pull out" of some employee the information needed to help him arrive at a satisfactory solution to his problem.

By its name and nature, counseling is a directive or a guidance activity. Many workers will come seeking help; others who need help will not come, but the foremen or a fellow worker may notify the counselor of the facts in the case. Under such conditions, approaching the individual concerned requires friendliness and tact. To carry directive counseling to its logical conclusion four steps should be observed:

1. The counselor gets all the facts;

2. He probes the facts for possible solutions;

3. Through consultation, he aids the counselee in fitting the facts together to arrive at a logical solution to his problem;

---

[7] Providing comfortable physical facilities within the plant should not be left to chance. "Here's Comfort at Work," *Modern Industry,* June 15, 1947, pages 18-20.

4. He checks back to make certain the counselee took the action needed to solve his problem.

The counseling service also offers employees help in a variety of ways that do not include guidance and direction. The maintaining of recreational and informational services are usually offered on a nondirective basis; those who see what they want help themselves, cafeteria-style. Health, safety, and induction programs, on the other hand, fall into the directive classification.

Through the process of interviewing, the chronic gripers are catalogued. New plaintiffs are heard with the openminded viewpoint that "maybe this fellow's got something there." If the presentation and subsequent interviews reveal the desire for action, the counselor has something to work on. Much is to be gained by listening. Many individuals will leave the interview well satisfied *to have presented their case* to someone who would listen sympathetically and attentively. This safety-valve technique is important in large organizations where the general attitude is an impersonal one.

Industry has done a good job with suggestion systems of one kind or another.[8] The most popular are those that require a few lines on a sheet of paper to tell the employee's ideas for doing some operation or process in a more simple and direct manner. Occasionally the foreman is the one who wants to hold back on the amount of the award to be given a worker for a suggestion. There are probably three good reasons for this: (1) Management has made foremen cost conscious through cost accounting procedures and records. Spending big money for suggestions, foremen reason, increases costs. (2) Being human, foremen tend to resent change; therefore, they play down the value of suggestions wherever change is involved. (3) To admit that a workman has turned up a valuable suggestion or improvement in a department over which a foreman has supervisory responsibility demands breadth of character beyond that possessed by the average indi-

---

[8] For an enlightening discussion of this topic read: Robert B. Shapiro, "$1000 for the Boss, $50 for Me," *Personnel Journal*, March, 1946, pages 338-344.

vidual.   Suggestion systems also provide a means of airing a good many gripes of the workers, too, although there are many individuals who do not want to put their opinions in writing.   Certain employees do not feel that they have a problem, but rather that the plant, the foreman, or a fellow worker has a problem that should be cleared up; the suggestion-box provides a ready outlet. The counselor should urge employees to record all details when some change in production technique is involved.   It would be unfortunate, indeed, to lose the point in writing the description of the suggested process or improvement.   Drawings and sketches are helpful in presenting ideas to the suggestion committee and in passing data up the line to top management.   Verbal suggestions are less likely to involve production techniques than they are to cover suggested improvements in supervision, services to workers, wage incentive plans, and the like.[9]

The Interview Technique

There is no lack of written material on the subject of interviewing.   The counselor uses the interview to attempt to get at facts that assist him in understanding the motives and drives of the counselee and the goals the counselee is attempting to attain.[10] How objective the counselor's objective is, and how well he conducts the interview, will depend upon how well trained he is in the techniques of interviewing.

To be successful, an interview should be conducted in private. The atmosphere should be one of calmness with no hint of impatience, curtness, or intolerance.   The interviewee is actually a guest of the interviewer, and as such he should be warmly welcomed and put at ease.   Few friendly meetings leave out such items as: "How have you been?   (Handshake)   Come on in! Give me your hat!   Have a chair . . ." etc.

[9] A newer development in suggestion systems is briefly treated in an article entitled: "Reward Problems, Not Suggestions," *Modern Industry,* August 15, 1947, page 128.

[10] Stanley G. Dulsky, "Vocational Counseling II—By Interview," *Personnel Journal,* May, 1941, pages 23-28.

The second step is to obtain "participation" by the interviewee. If the individual talks readily, the counselor may wish only to clear up some remote or obscure point through questioning. When the counselee fails to clarify his position or problem the counselor will have to raise questions that will draw explanatory answers. Questions that evoke "yes" and "no" answers will not reveal many details. Questions like the following stimulate participation. "Where were you . . . ? What did you do . . . ? When do you . . . ? How do you . . . ? Why do you . . . ? Who should . . . ?"

The third and final step involves satisfaction to the interviewee. If the interview has been highly satisfying to the individual he is likely to be enthusiastic enough to express his feelings openly with a smile and some word of commendation. If he is a stolid individual a question or two like the following may rouse him. "Which plan do you think will meet your need? What is your reaction to . . . ? When do you plan to . . . ?"

The counselor will want to follow-up the interview to determine if the individual was able to carry out the planned action and if the individual is satisfied with the results. Action which will directly affect the counselee may be taken by the counselor. When this is the case, the counselor must make certain that he performs his part of the bargain. Unless the interviewee has secured satisfaction as a result of the interview the time given over to it may have been wasted. Satisfaction, as used here, does not mean that the employee always "gets his way." He is entitled, however, to a satisfactory explanation of WHY he cannot hope to have his way in the matter.

Reporting Progress

Progress reports should be made to the personnel director as has been pointed out in Chapter 11, pages 157-158. There should also be a clear channel for reports to reach top management. Counseling is so closely tied in with industrial relations that reports of this kind should serve as a barometer of the feelings and attitudes of plant workers. The tenor of the counselor's report should reflect the degree to which personnel and supervisory practices are in balance.

Failure to make reports may result in the eventual elimination of the service as being of little value; failure on the part of top management to utilize salient facts presented in the progress report may result in a breakdown in the human relations program of the organization. While the rendering of interesting and succinct reports requires concentrated effort and may be considered boresome by unenthusiastic counselors, they are known to be vital to the satisfactory functioning of the program.

Correcting Weaknesses within the Counseling Program

If some service of the counseling program is suffering due to lack of personnel, lack of funds, inadequate counselors, or other factors, it should be included in the counselor's progress report so that steps may be taken to correct the undesirable situation and bring the service up to par. If an individual counselor fails to measure up to the required standards of his job, prompt action should be taken by top management. Additional in-service training may correct certain weaknesses but not all failures can be prevented. Those that do occur must be dealt with realistically. Disciplinary action would hardly seem in order in a counseling program, yet it is necessary at times.

A case to illustrate the necessity for taking corrective action is mentioned to give emphasis to the thought that even well adjusted counselors will on occasion overstep the bounds of good behavior. The assistant counselor involved conducted the testing and induction training of new employees, and her work was highly satisfactory. The workload was such that her services could not readily be dispensed with. About every three months this young woman would show up with a black eye. During the week or ten days it would take for the eye to clear up there was much office talk and a letdown in personnel department activity.

With the third recurrence of her black eye, the office staff was thrown into a generally hilarious state which took days to wear off. A frank discussion of the situation revealed that the girl, while divorced, still cared for her former mate. They would date occasionally, have a few cocktails, and she would come out of the affair with a bad eye. It seems that her former husband liked liquor and was increasingly difficult to manage when he had a few drinks.

The facts were placed in the woman's personnel folder along with a copy of a personally addressed notification to the effect that another disruption in office routine, if caused by the black eye, would result in her dismissal. Thus, one may see that the counseling service itself may have personnel problems that disrupt the service it is attempting to render. Regardless of where weaknesses lie, they should be eliminated promptly.

Keeping Abreast of the Movement

The counseling service and the personnel department library should be well stocked with the newest and the best literature in the field. As has been pointed out on page 205, every counselor should be encouraged to read and take notes. Personnel workers will want to belong to some professional organization. The annual conventions of the American Management Association offer the counselor an excellent opportunity to meet others in the personnel field. Many states have personnel associations sponsored by a university or some other institution. The counselor can get help and inspiration from belonging to such a group. Luncheon clubs offer still another opportunity to meet fellow counselors. In some localities, small groups of personnel workers have formed their own association for the purpose of exchanging ideas and information.

The individual who is interested in his work usually gets around to those meetings which keep him informed on current trends in the counseling movement. Counselors are urged to read extensively because much of what they are doing has not yet been crystallized in a well written book. What the counselor is expected to do crosses the field of several specialties. It is not as yet possible to pick up a single text that will give the answers to all problems.   To be on the mailing list of several good publishers helps to keep one informed on new books in the field and personnel magazines carry informative articles as well as announcements of new books.   Not all plants will permit counselors to attend professional meetings during working hours, and not all counselors desire the associations available at the local luncheon club.   This leaves the counselor with but one sure way of keeping abreast of the movement—that is to read! read! read! and to interpret the information found in various articles and books.

Questions

1. Indicate the job titles you would set up when initiating a counseling program in a plant employing 1000 male and 500 female workers.
2. Discuss the duties and responsibilities of the counselor:
   a) To management   c) To the personnel director
   b) To the supervisor   d) To the worker
3. How should the counselor be introduced?
4. What space and equipment does the counselor need?   Discuss.
5. How should the counseling program be publicized?
6. What are the types of services offered?   To whom?
7. Discuss the desirability of evaluating results.
8. Explain the difference between the human relations problems and the production problems that confront foremen and supervisors.
9. In terms of present economic and labor relations conditions and in order of importance to you, list the duties you would assign to a counselor.   Select items from pages 184-186.
10. What term summarizes the plant counseling function?

Bibliography

Cantor, Nathaniel, *Employee Counseling*, pages 7-28.   New York: Mc-Graw-Hill Book Co., 1945.

Trigg, Frances W., "The Job of the Industrial Counselor for Women," Federal Security Agency, U. S. Office of Education.   Washington 25, D. C.: Superintendent of Documents, Government Printing Office, 1944.

Report of Conferences for Industrial and Vocational Counselors, 1945. School of Vocational Education, Clemson College, Clemson, S. C.

THE number of counselors employed seems to dictate the need for an organizational pattern if an effective counseling program is to be provided. In few large plants will the personnel director find the time necessary to hear individual reports from counselors. The appointment of a chief counselor makes possible the fixing of responsibility, and provides a routine by which top management receives a composite report of counseling activities. This organizational detail should result in a more effective counseling program.

Co-ordinating and Directing the Work of Other Counselors

If a plant operates more than one shift, the chief counselor may find it advantageous to designate someone to serve as an assistant for these hours. Some plants insist that women counselors submit all reports to the chief woman counselor and that men counselors report only to chief male counselors. Local plant conditions may require this division of authority, but unless the need has been demonstrated, there is little reason for the practice. Any member of the counseling staff should be capable of reporting factual material of a medical, social, economic or technical nature to his or her supervisor. Workers, however, should be permitted to report to a counselor of their own sex for help with personal problems if this is their preference.

Subordinate counselors who feel a degree of timidity in reporting certain health and sanitary problems to their superior officers should seek the assistance of the plant nurse for advice, technical information, and the reassurance needed to make a satisfactory presentation. If Negroes are employed at the plant, a separate counseling staff should not be necessary to handle their problems. A counseling staff of isolated members is not desirable; all should work co-operatively, each telling substantially the same story under the same set of conditions.

The chief counselor must be fully cognizant at all times of the problems and the activities of the counselors under his direction.[1] He should make at least daily contact with his co-workers, and more frequently when the occasion demands. To co-ordinate and direct the activities of the counseling staff, the chief counselor should include some or all of the following activities in his daily routine:

1. Review and evaluate records and reports made by counselors.

2. Recommend changes that are necessary in the light of fluctuating plant conditions.

3. Hold regularly scheduled meetings with the counseling staff.

4. Seek to clarify all situations in terms of WHY.

5. Remove promptly all duplication, repetition, and overlapping of effort.

6. Exercise leadership and point the way for co-operative effort between foremen, supervisors, employees, and the counseling service.

The chief counselor should conduct his activities in a manner to deserve the respect of his subordinates. His attitude should be one of patience, tolerance, and helpfulness. Coolheadedness should permit him to direct successfully the efforts of others even in the face of difficult production conditions in the plant, troubled feelings of the employees, or any other unfortunate circumstances within the organization.

Acting as a General Consultant

In a plant of several hundred employees at least one counselor should be available at all times on the production floor. The counseling service should be as close to management as the tele-

---

[1] A review of the declared objectives of a personnel program at this point might be helpful. See: Lewis J. Johnson, "Personnel Philosophy," *Personnel Journal,* June, 1946, pages 42-49.

phone.   The counselor must work closely with members of other departments such as personnel, safety, timekeeping, health, and payroll.   A continually harmonious working relationship should exist between the counselor and the foremen and supervisors. The chief counselor must keep his records and reports in such condition that he can furnish immediate information and opinions to the various departments when they call for counselor services. He should have a thorough knowledge of the work force and should recommend changes that will create better working conditions and greater working efficiency.

Factual information obtained by the counseling service should be documented and tabulated in order to build records and make reports that will prove to be reliable and valid.   Through the presentation of factual material that stands up under pressure, the counselor and counseling service will gradually gain in stature. The counselor, in gathering facts, should take into account the opinions and thoughts of workers, but he must learn to withhold his own opinions.   The assembly of data and plotting trends on matters of wages, hours, bonus payments, absenteeism, tardiness, loans, co-operatives, credit unions, hospitalization, pensions, and a host of other similar matters will result in the counselor being considered the logical person to consult for reliable information on these subjects.   Statistics gathered by the counselor should serve a useful purpose in the counseling program.

Assisting in the Selection of Counselors

The chief counselor should exercise at least recommendatory power in the selection of additional counselors for his department. Wherever possible, the chief counselor should have full authority to review applications, interview, and select his counseling assistants.   It is only through having this power that a close-knit organization can be built up.   There should be no alarm expressed, however, over the fact that someone up-the-line must approve all appointments.[2]

---

[2] For a wholesome discussion of co-operation between the personnel department and management see: Garret L. Bergen, "War's Lessons in Personnel Service,"

If the basic aim of the program is to help employees with their problems, then the number of counselors to be selected will be determined by the size of the plant. Some counseling programs have been established to counsel employees *incidentally,* and management *directly.* In this plan, only one counselor might be required. The counselor might never be called upon to select assistants, yet he might be asked to name his successor in case of a change in his own employment.

Few people in the plant are in a better position to know of qualified prospective counseling material than the chief counselor. Most organizations have adequate employee personnel records which will give the "paper qualifications" of prospective counselors. Through contact with the individual, the chief counselor should be able to evaluate the personality and ability of his potential successor. Responsibility for the special investigation of counselors coming to the plant from other locations should fall to the chief counselor who will have to evaluate the emotional stability, the depth and warmth of personality, and the resourcefulness and objectivity of the applicant.

Maintaining Community Resources Guides

The chief counselor is responsible for obtaining information on community resources.[3] He has a further responsibility for maintaining a co-operative arrangement with other agencies. It is advisable, therefore, that he attend community activities and participate in professional meetings which keep abreast of the new developments in the community and enable him to serve the employees at his plant more effectively. Counselors should be aware of all community resources that might be used to aid employees in their adjustment to the job. Ability to become ad-

---

Personnel Service, July-August, 1945, pages 19-31. Published by the National Retail Dry Goods Association.
    [3] See: *Employment Counseling in the Public Employment Service,* Development of Directory of Community Agencies, War Manpower Commission, Bureau of Placement, Items 7180-7184. Washington, D. C.: Superintendent of Documents, Government Printing Office, September, 1944.

justed to the community is also important to employees, and the counselor who co-operates with other agencies in the community will have the best facilities at his command for assisting workers to make the necessary adjustments to plant and community environment.

Community resources guides should be developed by the counseling service for use as information directories. Personal contact should be made with the key person in the agency and the nature of the counselor's mission should be explained. Some brief statement of typical problems of the plant and its workers will give the agency a clearer viewpoint of the kind of help needed when service calls are made at a later date.

The counselor will want an understanding with his superior officer as to the extent that the affairs of the plant may be discussed in meetings outside the plant. There should be a willingness to exchange ideas on certain matters, but there will be a point beyond which plant matters will not be disclosed. The boundary should be clearly understood by the counselor. He should have well planned answers prepared when he reaches the outer limits of his authority to avoid creating an impression of non-co-operation with other agencies.

Frequent calls and referrals will keep the community resources guides up-to-date. The best way to keep the guide current is to use it! If three-by-five cards are used to record information on housing, loans, rehabilitation services and the like, one entry should be made on each card. These cards may be shuffled and reshuffled to meet any given set of conditions. If the cards are made up in duplicate form, one set may be alphabetized while the second set may be arranged to furnish clues to the services rendered. A card system permits the pulling of a given card and the replacement of one containing current information; files can be streamlined through the elimination of cards that have become obsolete, a convenient process contrasted with crossing off the names of agencies no longer in existence, or the writing in of names of newly created agencies.

On the back of each card the counselor may list the date and the nature of all contacts with that agency. This technique permits the making of corrections almost immediately. It is suggested that the duty of keeping the community resources guide up to date be assigned to a member of the counseling staff. Direct contacts with the agencies, and periodic reviews of telephone directories and personnel agency directories will assist in keeping the file up to date. Should the community lack services in certain fields, such as legal aid or health centers, the counselor may be able to work out arrangements for developing referral sources among lawyers, doctors, or credit establishments in the community.

The guides should be alphabetically indexed to cover federal, state, county, and local groups, as well as private organizations functioning in the community. The activity fields that should be included are education, employment, training, health, housing, veterans' services and welfare. Each card should contain the address, telephone number, name of the organization, administrative responsibilities, and the name of the person contacted. Community guides serve as a key for counselor contacts with other agencies and organizations, and are used as a source of information for directing a counselee not only to the correct agency, but to the specific person who will handle his problem.

An example of the use of the community guide in counseling would be the case of an individual seeking employment who has a vocational handicap that prevents his passing the physical examination given all applicants. The defect is one easily corrected and the applicant possesses skills that are needed by the plant. The community guide is referred to, and under the heading, State Board for Vocational Education, is found the Vocational Rehabilitation Division which provides corrective assistance to persons with vocational handicaps. Contact is made by telephone with one of the field workers and an appointment is made for the counselee. The individual is hospitalized; at a later date he is employed by the plant.

Counseling Reports

The chief counselor makes required reports to top management on the activities of his counseling staff.   To be effective, all reports should give specific facts and detailed information, but they should be briefed or summarized for quick reading by a busy executive.   It might be well to key the summary so that the details of any particularly cogent point can be located in the main factual presentation.

Good timing is essential to the effectiveness of a report.   For example, factual material on the underlying reasons for separations will be of a greater value if submitted at a time when the turnover rate is starting to increase.   Postponing the report until a reduction in force is being planned would render the entire effort a waste of time.   Reports that concern employees as members of labor unions might or may be made available to both management and the union steward for study and recommendation. However, the approval for the submission of such reports to persons or organizations other than plant management is a responsibility that rests with top management and not with the counselor.[4]

The counselor is cautioned about "hiding his light under a bushel" simply because management requires no report of his activities.   It is dangerous to assume that because everything seems to be moving along well that management is fully aware of the scope of the counseling job being done.   Concise reports should be prepared voluntarily and furnished to top management.

Orienting New Counselors

The chief counselor has a responsibility for the proper induction and orientation of other counselors in the organization. Steps to be included in the induction process are:

1. Explaining the plant organization and how the counselor fits into the management structure

---

[4] The matter of teamwork between management and its employees is of increasing importance.   Employees told "Why" as well as "How" tend to work more willingly in the team than those less well-informed.   "Tell 'em Why—as Well as How," *Modern Industry*, April 15, 1947, pages 67-78.

2. Explaining and showing counselors the physical layout of the plant and the personnel department

3. Introducing the counselors to co-workers, supervisors, and foremen

4. Explaining and discussing special practices and policies

5. Acquainting the counselor with all services offered to employees.

The orientation program requires considerably more time than does the induction process.   The new counselor may require some repetition of information and events to fix the accepted practices of the organization in his mind.   Certain activities will occur daily, others weekly, and others less frequently.   To describe an event that will take place on some distant date is to waste time in the telling.   Consequently, the orientation program should be spread over a period of time.   There is no reason to delay in getting off to a good start, however.   This may be done in the following manner:

1. Explain all the counselor's functions.

2. Inform the counselor of the rules and regulations he is supposed to observe.

3. Inform the counselor of the methods of counseling used in the establishment.

4. Point out the relationship of the counselor to the personnel department.

5. Clear up in the new counselor's mind all points as to authority on transfers, promotions, ratings, position classifications, separations, compensations, absenteeism, accident reporting, and disciplinary action.

6. Keep the counselor up to date on all new developments in personnel policies, practices, and procedures.

7. Provide the counselor with professional reading and encourage him to join professional organizations in his field.

8. Evaluate the work of the counselor in an objective manner and inform him of strong points while encouraging him to overcome weaknesses.

9. Make constructive suggestions that will result in an improved counseling service.

The First Day

After a careful induction period, certain steps may be followed in getting the counselor settled in his new surroundings. The method in which these steps are taken will give him some cues as to the orderliness with which the counseling department functions. The atmosphere should be one of ease rather than tenseness. Some steps to be followed in working with a counselor during the first day on the job include:

1. Taking the counselor to his assigned desk
2. Seeing that he is provided with filing space and sufficient office supplies to perform assigned duties; acquainting him with the procedure for obtaining supplies and other materials with which to work
3. Making assignments of clerical help and introducing the counselor to the secretary
4. Making certain that the counselor meets all persons in immediate supervisory positions who might contact the new counselor during the first week
5. Assisting the new counselor to make a detailed list of all duties; explaining the scope of these duties and fixing responsibilities
6. Helping the counselor to understand the system of records and reports in use
7. Pointing out the advantages of keeping a daily record sheet
8. Explaining any other details that will aid him in getting started with his first day's work.

The First Week

It is important that the new counselor does not get off to a hurried start. Time should be provided for him to assimilate material that will aid him in handling problems that come to him;

consequently some professional reading during working hours should be encouraged. It might be well to suggest that the reading should cover factual material on matters of current importance to the plant and that notes be taken, preferably in topical sequence. The counselor might be encouraged to arrange his notes so that he will have information on such matters as:

(1) suggestions for reducing absenteeism on Monday mornings; (2) suggestions for improving job-pride; (3) techniques that improve safety records; (4) aids that develop job-responsibility.

The new counselor should receive copies of all reading materials, notices, directives, and other communications that will make him feel he is part of the organization. He should also become familiar with the community resources guide. A proportionate share of the counseling work—employee inductions, for example—should be assigned during the first week on the job, so that he is eased gradually into the work routine.

The First Month

During the first month the process of orientation should have brought the new counselor face to face with increasingly difficult problems. His routine should be pretty well fixed in his mind, and his outlook should be expanding. At the end of the month, a period of evaluation and counseling on the following matters is suggested:

1. Discuss the new counselor's daily record of activities. Help him to analyze the different types of problems handled and the techniques employed.

2. Review with him his list of counselees. For example, if he counseled with ten people on tardiness, he will want to follow-up to determine what results were accomplished.

3. Review with him his list of duties, adding new ones to the list, or deleting those that are no longer needed or performed.

In addition to individual conferences with new counselors the chief counselor may:

1. Arrange to have all counselors meet for a discussion of problems that can be worked out through group action.

2. Discuss weaknesses in the program and seek suggestions for correcting known deficiencies.

3. Evaluate the performance of all counselors and help them to overcome weaknesses.

4. Devise ways and means for presenting examples of outstanding performance to the group so that it may set a pattern and prove to be a motivating force.

5. Where necessary, take disciplinary or corrective action to clear up any situation which has proved to be the result of mistaken judgment.

Summary

The plant with several counselors should assign the responsibility for maintaining counseling quality to the chief counselor. In addition to keeping top management informed of developments in the counseling program, the chief counselor may select other counselors, orient and supervise new counselors, contact outside agencies, and co-ordinate all counseling activity.

Questions

1. Under what set of conditions would a chief counselor be considered a necessary addition to a counseling staff?
2. Plan a program for a new counselor's first week on the job.
3. State at least five activities the counselor should consider at the end of the first month.
4. Explain a counseling staff of "isolated units."
5. Select one of the chief counselor's suggested daily activities and discuss it in terms of its importance to the entire program.
6. Tell what should be done with factual information collected by the counseling service.
7. What purpose do community resources guides serve?
8. Name the steps involved in orienting new counselors.
9. Make a simple line chart showing your concept of the relationships

existing between the counseling service, the personnel department, foremen, managers, and workers.

10. List five duties of the chief counselor.

Bibliography

Dimock, Marshall Edward, *The Executive in Action*. New York: Harper & Brothers, 1945.

Morgan, Howard K., *Industrial Training and Testing*. New York: McGraw-Hill Book Company, 1945.

Schell, Erwin Haskell, *The Technique of Executive Control*. New York: McGraw-Hill Book Company, 1946.

Bingham, Walter Van Dyke and Moore, Bruce Victor, *How to Interview*. New York: Harper & Brothers, 1934.

AMONG the features to be considered when setting up a program of counseling are the desirable goals of attainment. After a program has been in operation a month, the actual achievements should be compared with the objectives to determine how well or how poorly the accomplishments measure up to the desired aims. This process of evaluation not only gives a measurement of what has been done, but also indicates what remains undone and where greater effort should be concentrated.

The Counselor Evaluates the Program

Evaluation is a process of comparison. Three key points are involved in the process of evaluating the counseling program. Point one is the goal or objective set for the service. There is a tendency to fail to set any goal of attainment. Under conditions of this kind, the program will drift aimlessly. Management will have few ideas relative to where the program should be headed, and unless the "gripes" get long and loud, management is not apt to know what results are being obtained.[1]

Point two in the evaluation process is a review of results. Results may be immediate or long-term. Usually, immediate results are those that take care of the problem of the hour. The long-term results may be only partially accomplished at any one time, yet these piecemeal accomplishments bring the program ever

---

[1] Various techniques may be utilized to discover what your employees are thinking. "What are Your Workers Thinking?" *Modern Industry,* April 15, 1947, pages 40-44.

nearer its ultimate goals or objectives. This evaluation should tell us whether we need to exert a little or a lot more effort to reach our objective. We should know whether we are failing or succeeding in our attempts to render an acceptable service.

Point three is the individual or committee making the evaluation. The chief counselor, the personnel director, or a management-worker committee may check the program for results. If the evaluation is made upon a factual basis rather than upon hearsay and gripes, the report is less likely to be colored by opinions. If their evaluation indicates that the results being obtained are not satisfactory, then adjustments are in order.

The counselor should also consider developing a personal appraisal sheet to evaluate his own performance. This sheet may be used to compare personal growth with the achievements of the entire program. The counselor's rating sheet, to be of greatest value, should be prepared in an objective manner as if he were gauging the performance of a fellow worker. Here again, desirable goals of attainment should be compared with the results achieved and the differences carefully noted.

The evaluation process, which should be carried out in privacy and without petty interruptions, should be a step by step review of the entire program.[2] Activities pressing for attention should be flagged for immediate action. A second matter is that of carry-over items from previous evaluations. Any item in the spotlight for action from a previous month's evaluation should be carefully watched for results. If the program has failed to correct known weaknesses, the counselor should down-grade himself in supervisory ability. The number of items carried over from month to month, however, should be small. Most carry-over problems should be of relatively minor importance; major items must receive prompt attention and satisfactory solution.

---

[2] Some counselors will be interested in the over-all subject of job evaluation as applied to modern industrial production plants. For such a description the following article is suggested: "What's New in Job Evaluation?" *Modern Industry*, June 15, 1947, pages 44-47.

Review the Record

It is considered good practice for the counselor to study records and reports in search of significant trends. If, for example, after grouping reports and analyzing figures on absenteeism it is determined that housing or transportation is causing a disruption or slowdown in production, immediate investigation is in order. A series of questions may give the needed clues to the solution of the problem.[3] What constructive improvements could be made? How much can absenteeism be reduced through applying this or that remedy? List suggested remedies. Who in the organization might be best qualified to institute the remedy? When should the new plan be put into effect?

Analyze the Situation

After raising questions and setting down logical answers, the counselor should probe the material for the specific techniques that will assist in solving the problem. Clues which reveal possible preventive measures are of greatest value, yet their application in some situations may not yield immediate, tangible results. The counselor will have to decide whether preventive measures should be instituted which will eliminate the undesirable end results.

Evaluation also should be made to determine appropriate action. If further improvement is needed, the action to clear up these items should be swift and sure. Evaluation should determine how the over-all program has helped management, and how specific counseling services have aided workers.

A program that is permitted to drift will eventually get so far off a given course that it may be easier to abandon the whole undertaking rather than to get it back on the beam. To avoid this condition, the counselor should institute a definite schedule for evaluating his entire program. Weaknesses should be cor-

---

[3] There are six questions presently being used to test how effectively employees are working. Gauging the skill and effort of a worker, known as "leveling," is described briefly in "Six Ways to Judge Worker Performance," *Modern Industry,* January 15, 1947, pages 96-98.

rected promptly and a plan of action outlined to overcome recurring difficulties.

FACTORS TO CONSIDER WHEN EVALUATING THE COUNSELOR'S ASSISTANCE TO MANAGEMENT

1. EMPLOYEE MORALE

The Appraisal

What improvements have been suggested to management for improving working conditions?

How have policies been altered or improved?

Has production increased?   Decreased? [4]

What evidences are there that production has improved in quality?

What department shows the greatest number of gripes? Least number?

Where in the plant has there been the most conclusive evidence indicating an improvement in morale?

What other evidences are there of improved or lowered morale?

The Key to Improvement

Review the handling of all gripes or complaints.

Determine the source of recurring problems.

Aid supervisors whose records indicate the need for assistance in human relations problems.

Make certain that employees know the reasons WHY when announcements that affect them are made.

Time the posting of notices so that complaints are reduced to a minimum.

2. PLANT SAFETY

The Appraisal

Have the most improved mechanical devices been installed?

Is appropriate safety clothing being worn throughout the plant?

---

[4] The importance of incentives to increase production cannot be overlooked. See: "Winning Workers to Productivity," *Modern Industry,* December 15, 1946, pages 49-64.

Does the number of eye accidents justify an order requiring the wearing of goggles throughout the plant?

Is the accident frequency rate of the plant in keeping with the industry as a whole?

Is the frequency rate increasing or decreasing?

Are employees informed of the trend in the frequency rate by bulletins or other means?

Is the severity rate increasing or decreasing?

Are departments competing with each other for better safety records?

The Key to Improvement

Work with the Safety department to improve the plant's safety record.

Review the safety engineer's records.

Spot departments with the best as well as poorest safety records.

Plan competition and incentives to stimulate departmental improvement.

Investigate accident-prone individuals and offer suggestions to top management to overcome difficulties.

3. Major Problems—Absenteeism, Turnover, etc.

The Appraisal

Has factual material been gathered to indicate a trend?

What are the underlying causes of the difficulties?

Would the changing of some plant policy or procedure clear up the situation?

How does the plant record compare with those of other plants?

Has an analysis been made to spot particular departments where weaknesses are prevalent?

When problems occur are there individuals who are responsible for effecting prompt settlement?

The Key to Improvement

Utilize the facilities of the State Employment Service in gathering data for comparative purposes.

Interest management in improving or correcting conditions that cause major problems, i.e., wages, working conditions, quality of supervision, etc.

Investigate practices of other plants having better records and determine reasons for their success.

Make use of training facilities in the community to improve skill of supervisors in handling human relations situations.

Determine whether responsibility can or cannot be assigned to some specific individual for the settlement of problems.

4. RECORDS AND REPORTS

The Appraisal

Have counseling records and reports been complete and accurate?

What trends have been spotted and highlighted for management?

What conclusions may be drawn from the trends?

Have suggested improvements been given to management?

How can records and reports be briefed and simplified?

The Key to Improvement

Give management the facts.

Make summaries of reports for quick reading.

Use graphs, charts, and other visual aids.

Make suggestions, based upon facts, that will overcome known *weaknesses* in the counseling program.

Keep management aware of the thoughts and actions of the workers.

Attempt to weigh and evaluate the feelings and attitudes of workers, foremen, and supervisors.

FACTORS TO CONSIDER WHEN EVALUATING THE COUNSELOR'S ASSISTANCE TO SUPERVISORS

1. THE NUMBER OF SUPERVISORS HELPED

The Appraisal

How many supervisors have been contacted?

Have only those who co-operate with the program been contacted?

Why have certain problems recurred?

What attempts have been made to sell the program to those who are non-co-operative?

What factors outside the counseling program itself tend to impede the relations between the counselor and the supervisors?

The Key to Improvement

Hold conferences with supervisors to determine what help they need and want.

Concentrate more effort on selling the program to those who are not convinced that the counselor can be of assistance.

Request management to cite examples of improved human relationships brought about by the counseling program, to tell supervisors of its confidence in the work of the counselor, and to urge supervisors to make full use of the service.

Try to spot weaknesses and work out helpful solutions.

Make certain that whatever supervisory training is offered by the training department is of the highest quality, geared to the needs of the group, and acceptable to those involved.

Strengthen the position of the supervisor by working with him and through him.

By your actions convince the supervisors that you are a member of their team.

2. Ways in Which Supervisors Have Been Helped

The Appraisal

What improvements have been suggested?

What results were obtained from suggestions made to supervisors?

In what way did the suggestions help the production record of the supervisor?

What human relations problems were solved for the supervisor with his co-operation?

What remains to be done to render greater or more effective service to foremen?

How do the accomplishments shown in this evaluation compare with previous reports?

What weak spots in the program have been overcome?

How has timing aided in matters where the supervisor has sought help?

Where have preventive measures been suggested?

The Key to Improvement

Make comparative studies to discover weaknesses and strong points in supervision.

Build up weak supervisors through training in human relations.

Try to time the action taken so that recurrence of the problem is avoided.

Continue to isolate areas where difficulties arise at regular intervals.

Seek help from other departments and top management on problems beyond the scope of your duties or capacities.

FACTORS TO CONSIDER WHEN EVALUATING THE COUNSELOR'S ASSISTANCE TO EMPLOYEES

1. WORKER DISSATISFACTIONS—List each situation and submit it to pertinent questions such as the following:

The Appraisal

Do the facts bear out the contentions of the worker? [5]

What preventive measures have been instituted to ward off additional problems?

How many workers in the department have reported the same conditions?

Why has the supervisor failed to take corrective action?

Who else should have taken action?

In what way can conditions be improved?

Has the worker been told WHY changes and improvements can or cannot be made?

The Key to Improvement

Study the records carefully.

Take prompt action wherever possible.

Tell the worker what action is contemplated or what action has been taken.

Tell the worker WHY if no action can be taken.

Attack the cause not the symptoms.

Think in terms of preventive action when making adjustments.

---

[5] In the matter of handling one type of worker dissatisfaction see: "Handling Work-load Grievances," *Modern Industry*, March 15, 1947, page 39.

Follow-up to make certain that the worker feels he has been helped.

Don't depend upon someone else to follow through—make certain yourself.

Getting Worker Reaction

Since samples of worker reaction to the quality of the counseling program may not be forthcoming in sufficient volume to be a reliable gauge for measuring the quality of the counseling program, definite techniques must be used for getting worker reactions.   These techniques involve seeking facts rather than waiting for information to reach the counselor. Not all information about the program should be gathered conversationally because useful facts are sometimes lost or distorted in the telling.   Opportunities for the workers to list or to write out their evaluations should also be provided.

House organs make it possible to run a questionnaire which will poll worker opinion on the quality of the plant counseling work. The check-list idea seems to work best, although an occasional completion-type statement to be made by workers can furnish useful information. For example, employees may be asked to complete a sentence in 25 words or less, similar to the currently popular soap ad contests: "I think the counseling program is helpful to all employees because——————" or, "I think the counseling program could be improved by——————." Workers will be stimulated to offer suggestions if a prize is offered for the best answer. The answers give the counselor and the personnel department a chance to improve as well as publicize the program.

The check-list idea on the other hand, provides some ten to twenty items for workers to evaluate in terms of excellent, good, fair, or poor. Such an evaluation is more objective and gives the counselor an opportunity to discover where plant employees feel that the program is "missing the boat." Prompt, corrective action may clear up a widespread feeling of dissatisfaction. These check lists should be used once or twice a year for best results, since too frequent repetition will tend to reduce their effectiveness. Conversely, when used too infrequently, the counseling program may be seriously out of balance before corrective measures are taken.

A third method that may be used in securing worker reaction is to urge greater use of the plant suggestion system. Employee suggestions can lead the way to improved counseling services and indicate new activities desired by the workers. Adoption of practical ideas gives workers the feeling that they have a voice in the formation of plant personnel policies. Possibly, suggestions and complaints require different treatment. If employee ideas and suggestions receive prompt action, however, fewer and fewer complaints will be forthcoming. Many suggestion systems fail because of the time lapse between submission of the idea and putting it into practice.

Progressive management will want to keep informed of new developments and new ideas being propounded by employees. A tabulation sheet recording the number of times an idea has been suggested will eliminate the passing to top management of crackpot schemes that are neither workable nor desirable. All ideas that can be put to work should be transmitted to the top for approval, and then promptly put into action. Workers should be told in advance of the changes to be made, the source of the ideas, and the resultant benefits to employees.

Many of the criticisms offered will give management the clues needed in finding a solution to an unsatisfactory plant practice. Modifications and counterproposals frequently can be timed so that serious trouble in the plant is avoided. The counselor will find that only dynamic, progressive management is willing to keep an ear to the ground to find out what the employees are thinking and feeling.[6] The counselor will learn also that it takes an alert and active individual to gather *thoughts* and *attitudes* and in-

---

[6] Executives must be trained to look the situation squarely in the eye and be willing to make the needed changes. For a further discussion of uses of the suggestion box, read: "Training Executives in Executive Skills," *Modern Industry,* March 15, 1947, pages 45-48.

terpret them in a manner that will provide workable plans for management to use in maintaining harmonious personnel relationships.

Summary

An evaluation of the counseling program should be made periodically to discover weaknesses and dissatisfactions before too long a time has elapsed. The counselor may make his own evaluation or he may enlist the aid of supervisors, workers, and his superior, the personnel manager. Prompt remedial action is suggested as a means of avoiding the more serious difficulties likely to develop if faults remain uncorrected. The alert counselor may wish to evaluate his personal performance to determine how well it meets the needs of the organization.

Evaluation is a modern method utilized to discover worthwhile items in a going program and to determine the exact point at which improvements should be made. It should eliminate the common faults involved in the "hit-or-miss" and "trial-and-error" tactics of letting things drift. Evaluation is an objective, dynamic method of finding out what and where the trouble is, rather than a passive method of letting trouble come to the surface before recognizing that there may be management inadequacies.

Questions

1. Why should the counselor set goals of attainment for himself within the objectives set by top management?
2. How do you evaluate activities to determine accomplishments?
3. Discuss the process of analyzing a situation.
4. Discuss the appraisal of worker-dissatisfaction and the improvement of employee morale.
5. Discuss the factors related to appraisal and improvement of major problems.
6. Discuss the factors related to appraisal and improvement of record-keeping and reports.
7. Discuss the factors related to appraisal and improvement of counselor assistance to supervisors.

8. Why is the factor of employee morale important to management?
9. What is the value of obtaining the workers' reactions to management?
10. Discuss methods of securing the workers' reactions and the value of follow-up.

Bibliography

Carey, H. H., "Consultative Supervision; Technique for Ending Strife Between Management and the Man at the Machine," *Nation's Business,* April, 1937, Vol. 25, page 44.

Evans, J. J. Jr., *A Program for Personnel Administration,* pages 40-48. New York: McGraw-Hill Book Co., 1945.

Jager, Harry A., and Zeran, Franklin R., "Community Adult Counseling Centers," Federal Security Agency, U. S. Office of Education, Vocational Division, Washington, D. C., 1945. *Occupations,* the Vocational Guidance Journal, February, 1945. 525 West 120th Street, New York 27, N. Y.

Knowles, Asa S., and Thomson, Robert D., *Management of Manpower,* pages 137-143, 204. New York: The Macmillan Co., 1943.

"Factors Affecting Employee Morale," *Monthly Labor Review,* July, 1939, Vol. 49, pages 96-97.

During World War II, counseling contributed greatly to the reduction of absenteeism and turnover—an important factor in the maintenance of continuously high levels of production. Many individuals obtained their initial concept of a management-worker team from their contacts with the plant counselor. In industry, mass production and the pressure of turning out ever-increasing quantities of war goods led to the pyramiding of staffs. Accelerated hiring in all categories made necessary the use of large numbers of untrained supervisory personnel.

Putting the New Techniques to Work

With the war experience behind us and many challenging problems ahead, the counselor must be ever alert to new techniques and devices. The development of new methods makes it necessary to devote greater attention to planning. Improvements in services already being offered and the addition of new services challenge the counselor.[1] In the field of human relations the need has never been greater than at present for a service that aids management and assists workers with their common problems. Because human relations problems are dynamic, the counselor, in order to do a consistently satisfactory job, must keep the following factors in mind:

---

[1] Several universities have established personnel relations courses to aid the counselor and other members of plant personnel departments in becoming acquainted with modern trends in the field of human relations. "Personnel Research at Ohio State," Personnel Research Board of Ohio State University; *Personnel Journal,* November, 1945, pages 197-200.

1. Work with counselees as you find them. Start where they are and help them to help themselves.

2. Try to discover what the counselees wish to accomplish.

3. Help counselees to decide what pathway they wish to take to arrive at a satisfactory solution to the problem. The individual must decide. The counselor must not dictate.

4. Have the individual select a time to start work on his problem that will yield satisfactory results to him.

5. Suggest several possible courses of action. Have the individual weigh and decide upon a course of action.

6. Give information and offer suggestions when it appears that a problem can be met satisfactorily. Probe the situation for additional facts if the solution seems obscure.

7. Get counselees to view the situation realistically. Avoid over- or undershooting the goals of accomplishment.

8. Offer suggestions that tend to strengthen the individual's self respect.

Most going programs owe much of their success to the confidence that individuals have placed in them. This spirit of trust places great responsibility on the counselor and should make him doubly cautious that employees, superintendents, and management do not lean upon *him* to the exclusion of *healthy self-reliance*. Several plans of action may be offered by the counselor, but selection of one plan to the exclusion of others should be strictly up to the individual. The counselee is considered to be the person most competent to decide which plan of action will best meet his or her needs. It is not desirable for the person with the problem to be prevented from assuming the responsibility in making the choice of a plan.

Counselors must develop a sound, basic philosophy when dealing with human relations problems. There are many pitfalls into which the uninitiated may stray. The following suggestions may serve as guideposts for a successful program:

1. Logical reasoning, while highly desirable in a counselor, should play a lesser role than sentiment, emotion, social pressure,

or desires.   Too often, counselors think *only* in terms of logical reasoning while counselees may be motivated by urges, desires, and emotions.

2. Counselors must have or must develop a pleasing personality capable of attracting individuals and inviting relaxation and constructive thinking.

3. Many individuals who come to the counselor are attempting to play a false role in the game of life. Counselors should attempt to see behind the mask these people wear and to understand the end results that the "character" is trying to attain.

4. Long-term values are hard to clarify for individuals. We must frequently compromise with the immediate results to obtain a portion of the long-term values for the counselee.

5. Through experience the counselor learns which approach to use and when a given technique can be used to advantage.   There are times when the counselor should direct and guide an interview; on other occasions the counselee should be required to take the initiative.

6. Unwise, inadequate, and poorly timed treatment by the counselor can create recurring problems that eventually result in a complete breakdown of the individual's self reliance.

The challenge to counselors is multiphased and will increase with the size of the plant and the complexity of the supervision.[2] We have attempted to point out that the prime responsibility of counseling is that of aiding individuals and groups to solve their problems satisfactorily and to make the necessary, desirable adjustments to their jobs and environment. The relationship between high morale and job pride are so close that many plants could, figuratively, measure morale in terms of material spoilage. Morale is determined by numerous factors. The wording of a posted notice or the expressed displeasure of a grouchy foreman may seriously disrupt production schedules. The ability to solve

---

[2] There is a growing need for stronger personnel departments. The crux of this situation is discussed by: Forrest H. Kirkpatrick, "Better Personnel Administration," *Personnel Journal,* December, 1945, pages 231-238.

or mitigate the effects of such influences offers unlimited possibilities to those who understand human behavior.

Normal individuals desire to live useful, satisfying lives. Most workers are desirous of making a worthwhile contribution to better community living. Occasionally the counselor's advice will be sought by an individual who is trying to get back on the "right track" that leads to usefulness and community respect. The guidance supplied to such an individual may strengthen his self-respect or it may lead to new depths. Almost like the flip of a card hope may be restored or destroyed. The course of action suggested by the counselor will not always be an easy one, and the counselor's choice may be still more difficult to make; where human values are concerned the decision is seldom a simple one.

To understand what makes a worker "cuss out" a foreman who is known to be fair places the counselor squarely in the middle of the complex study of attitudes, ambitions, desires, drives, motives, urges, conflicts and frustrations. The literature of psychology and sociology is available at all public libraries, and courses are provided by universities and evening schools throughout the nation. Many of the leading universities are also prepared to give adequate courses by correspondence. The counselor whose background includes a knowledge of psychology and sociology is better prepared to understand why people behave as they do.

When management establishes a counseling program, it expects tangible results. The counselor must meet this challenge by giving assistance to all members of the organization. It is not likely that supervisors and managers will need frequent guidance and counsel on personal matters, but they may need factual data on trends, worker reactions, personnel practices, and the effect of policies on workers.

The counselor must develop and maintain a philosophy towards living that sets an example for those in supervisory positions.[3] He should radiate a buoyancy, vitality, and alertness that will

---

[3] Quentin W. File, "Are Management's Views of Supervision Faulty?" *Personnel Journal,* January, 1946, pages 242-254.

place him among those considered to be well adjusted mentally and physically. A considerate, friendly attitude toward those in difficulty and all fellow workers will clearly demonstrate the fact that the proper attitude towards life pays off in industrial relations and supervisory work. Deceitfulness, retaliation, cunning, and make-believe have no place in the counselor's repertoire. His honesty and integrity should be above reproach.

The counselor, to be of greatest value to counselees, should always have available sufficient information to answer honestly and intelligently all questions that are raised. Information not on hand should be obtained promptly from appropriate sources, see pages 199-200. The community's resources should be well known to those doing the counseling job. Efficiently catalogued information about the plant and the community provides an effective tool for the counselor in his contact and referral activities.

Understanding the Plant and Its Product

It is surprising to note how many workers and how many management representatives look upon industry as a place to *get* something. Actually, plants are in business to make a profit by producing goods that are needed by, and useful to, mankind. Service should be the objective of the individual, and the individual should be made aware of the fact that service is also a goal of business. The plant that fails to serve a useful purpose in society eventually passes out of existence.

Another important goal of industry is uninterrupted production.[4] For many years industry has been striving to produce superior products at progressively lower costs to the consuming public. The counselor can readily secure from the available sales data information that will show trends in prices along with the improvements of the product that have taken place over the years. The counselor who understands these trends and presents

---

[4] "What's Happening to Productivity?" *Modern Industry,* November 15, 1946, pages 49-64.

them to workers through the medium of posters, brochures, and bulletins will tend to dispel the notion that a plant serves no purpose but to make a profit for its stockholders.

Workers should be made aware of the fact that what they produce must compete on the open market for the needed sales volume to pay wages, operating, and material costs and, if there is anything left, to pay dividends. The real history of dividends paid should be an open book to the counselor. If dividends have been good throughout the years, workers should be encouraged to invest their earnings in the company. Much has been lost in neglecting to make workers a partner in the business by offering them shares of stock (at current market prices, of course). The attitude of many workers changes materially when they invest a few dollars in the company's stock.

Where profits have been small, workers may be advised of that fact, also. If enough workers can be persuaded to become shareholders in the organization, it may be possible to step up production to new, higher levels, improving the position of the plant, returning better wages to workers, and permitting better returns on their stock investments. Dividends of few companies exceed six per cent, yet many employees would quote figures several times that percentage if asked for an off-hand opinion. It is up to the counselor to know the truth about profits and strive to present the real facts to workers. The following illustrations appeared in Thompson Products, Inc., Annual Report to Employees.

The counselor must know the plant from the standpoint of the supervisory staff. The challenge lies in being able to devise corrective measures to overcome weaknesses more or less painlessly while reinforcing the good features of existing personnel practices. In too many organizations lack of training is the cause of weak spots in the supervisory staff. The counselor must not only know what is wrong, but he must have plans that will overcome these weaknesses. Plans to be acceptable must be attainable and within the scope of plant practices and policies.

The new counselor must be thoroughly familiar with established

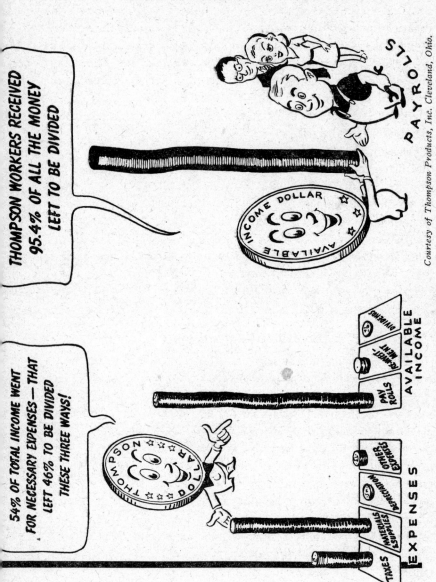

Courtesy of Thompson Products, Inc. Cleveland, Ohio.

GRAPHIC AIDS help the workers to visualize that what they produce must compete for a sales volume sufficient to pay wages and all other costs.

practices, policies, and procedures of the plant because these items are channel markers in the stream of progress that point the way in getting a job done.   The counselor who does not know and understand the circumscribed area within which he can and should function may find himself in over his head.   Most plants have their regulations in printed form and the material usually may be had for the asking.

Occasionally, however, the counselor may have to stop, look, and listen in order to learn what is considered to be acceptable practice.   Individuals moving from one plant to another are likely to assume that similar practices prevail in the new location and consequently they err by taking too many things for granted. Another error is that of trying to introduce practices from the old plant into the new.   Usually, ways of doing things are pretty well fixed.   Unless a directive "from the top" is issued to change a practice, the counselor should seek to bring about needed and desirable changes in a careful and gradual manner.

Knowing the Community

Learning about the community is a real challenge to the new-comer.   Individuals who have lived in a locality for some time usually have several contacts that help in getting acquainted with persons, departments, agencies and situations.   The counselor should not consider that "getting acquainted" is difficult, for frequently it is a pleasant experience.   Membership in one or more associations or clubs makes a good point for the entering wedge. Joining a church may also be the solution to making friends quickly when arriving in a community where primary contacts are of paramount importance in being accepted professionally.   Participation in community activities—political, recreational, educational, or spiritual—all provide splendid avenues for getting acquainted.

Some counselors feel that they know their community so well that they do not get around to various offices often enough to keep informed of changes.   Staff members and key employees in agencies and plants of the community do not remain static. To keep abreast of these personnel changes, the counselor should make calls at regular intervals. This is particularly true in situations where the plant counselor makes frequent referrals to agencies for services of a welfare nature.

Adequate knowledge of the community demands more than an awareness that somewhere there are a few public officials looking after the health and employment of the unfortunate. In fact, few public agencies perform only a single function these days. For a counselor to send a counselee to an agency or to a person whose duties are understood vaguely might result in embarrassment to the individual being referred and to the plant counselor himself. Counselees have even been referred to persons no longer connected with specific services! When the counselor has up-to-the-minute information about the agencies in the community, embarrassment for all concerned is eliminated.

Knowing Laws Affecting Worker Welfare

The counselor is confronted with the problem of understanding the many federal, state, and local laws that affect the welfare of employees. We have in recent years learned to rattle off the titles and numbers of certain federal laws. Public Laws 346 and 16 are of prime importance to the counselor because they cover, respectively, the provisions of the Servicemen's Readjustment Act of 1944 (G.I. Bill of Rights) and the Veteran Rehabilitation Program.[5]

In addition to the statutes as passed by Congress there are also various rulings, opinions, interpretations, and decisions handed down by the courts, boards, departments, and attorneys. Many federal laws affect the activities of counselors and supervisors, consequently they should be acquainted with the statutes and interpretations in order to avoid violations that would place the

---

[5] For a discussion of the need for counseling returning veterans read: Frederick W. Novis, "Reemployment Counseling," *Personnel Journal,* November, 1945, pages 183-191.

plant at a disadvantage. To assist companies and individuals in keeping up to date on this great volume of material, Prentice-Hall, Inc., publishes a looseleaf Labor Service that is all-inclusive and kept up to date by replacement pages sent out periodically. Its research staff furnishes the basic Act to Service subscribers as soon as it becomes a law. Recommendations are given frequently to guide the employer in application of the law to his own business. Later, when decisions and interpretations are handed down, these, too, are supplied to subscribers. This service is invaluable to employers, personnel departments and counselors in performing their duties effectively. In connection with the Taft-Hartley Act (formerly the Wagner Act), for example, management should be fully informed as to the rights of labor to bargain collectively, the meaning and definition of unfair labor practices, management's prerogatives under the Law, and the functions of the National Labor Relations Board. Recent labor legislation offers the counselor a challenge as well as an opportunity to function constructively within the structure and framework of the various Federal acts. The counselor should realize that the plant must have accurate, supportable facts to back up the foreman or supervisor in cases where a reprimand has been given, a transfer or demotion or discharge made, or a warning offered. Labor relations authorities usually suggest that the facts include:

1. Evidence that no attempt has been made to violate the spirit or letter of the Federal Act

2. Written reports covering details of action taken

3. Accurate records indicating that the employee had been informed of the exact point at which he had been failing

4. Records to prove that the employee had been given an opportunity to improve his weaknesses

5. Information to indicate that some official of the union had been informed of the contemplated action before it was taken.

In addition to these brief comments on fair labor practices as outlined in the Taft-Hartley Act, there are other statute provisions and interpretations covering the hiring, firing, and treatment of employees. The counselor should also acquaint himself with the labor statutes of the state in which he is employed.[6] State laws on child labor, apprenticeship, safety, wages and hours (to mention a few) vary, and it is a fallacy to assume that knowledge of the laws in one provides adequate understanding of the laws in a neighboring state.

Understand the Job Opportunities of the Plant

Too little is known about the effects of promotion upon morale. Much research on this phase of industrial relations is needed. It is believed that if employers knew fully the effects of promotion upon worker morale, more plants would provide progression sequences to advance workers within the organization. The counselor may or may not be in a position to do much about studying the effects of promotion upon morale; he is in a position, however, to inspect job analyses carefully to determine where progression sequences are possible. He can publicize these opportunities and thereby convince employees of the desirability of remaining with the company. To be most effective for both management and workers, promotion and transfer policies should be scientifically determined and agreed upon by both parties.

Knowledge of the job opportunities in the plant affords two distinct points for strengthening the counseling program. First, the counselor will understand better the advancement possibilities for workers—a strong selling or bargaining point when dealing with a worker who is unhappy, dissatisfied, or "in a rut." The information is also vital in selling all workers on the idea that the plant offers opportunities to those with a willingness to work and a desire to get ahead.

The counselor should realize that there is useful knowledge to be gained in studying plant jobs, payroll schedules, and employment sequences. Another outcome might be the appointment of

---

[6] Merely knowing the laws covering labor situations is not always sufficient; understanding the official interpretations is often of greater value. Frank Rising, "Whose Government Is It?" *The Saturday Evening Post*, July 5, 1947, page 120.

the counselor to a key management position should he know of a vacancy.

Understanding the Science of Counseling

The employee who is a "square peg in a round hole" in job adjustment problems will show up at the counselor's desk. Understanding how square pegs fail to get placed in square holes is to realize the hit-and-miss job placement techniques of many plants. The counselor needs to know the processes involved in matching job requirements with worker capacities and interests. It is important to bear in mind that the *ability* to perform is one thing and the *desire* to perform is quite another. Economic conditions force many people to select occupations that are unsuited to them. These workers may be capable of top-notch performance, but because they dislike their work thoroughly, they are not producers.

The counselor should understand interviewing and selection problems and should evaluate plant hiring practices in the light of what is considered the best of personnel practices. High turnover, worker dissatisfaction, and an excessive number of requests for transfer may be traced back to poor or inadequate employment practices.

The use of tests and testing devices to evaluate what the worker has done in the past and to determine hidden or latent skills and abilities should be more fully understood by counselors and other personnel workers. Both attitudes and aptitudes should be measured to determine where individuals may be placed to be happy in their employment as well as consistent in their output. Tests that reveal the job preferences of the individual tend to speed up the adjustment process. Testing programs that do no more than yield scores are of little value. The interpretation of test scores and test results is not a layman's task. For best outcomes, the person interpreting the scores should have the background necessary to give reasonably accurate prognosis based upon the factual data revealed by the tests.

The counselor should be strategically situated in the management structure where he can assist in the prevention of break-downs in the human relations line between workers and management, supervisors and management, and supervisors and workers. He should be responsible for advising foremen on "how to inform employees of their progress." The counselor, through reference to an individual's personnel file, can notify the foreman of a worker's past record. In matters of safety, leadership, and loyalty, the counselor can pass along words of commendation. Annual safety awards provide one means of publicly informing employees as to their achievements. Some plants present awards for years of service which tend to impress new workers with the fact that management recognizes the desirability of continuous, loyal service.

Spot newspaper stories commending workers for unusual performance may be released or received by the personnel department and the counselor selected to offer management's congratulations. Regardless of who conveys them, however, the counselor will be in a position to publicize the facts. Items of outstanding performance should be recognized while the situation is still "hot." Service and contributions above and beyond the line of routine duties is recognized by the military and other groups with medals and prizes. Industry in attempting to sell itself to employees should do no less.

The counselor, as the liaison officer between management and workers, will want to keep employees informed of changes that affect the latter. Notices of this kind should be posted as early as possible to give all persons concerned an opportunity to make the necessary personal adjustments. Some plants have conducted timing tests and are convinced that they have determined an ideal formula for posting notices; but no rule can be laid down since timing strategy varies between plants. This statement does not mean that notices posted at the last moment (to make it impossible for opponents to protest) are desirable. Union agreements usually stipulate the amount of time that a notice shall be posted before a new order will take effect. Whenever possible it should be the rule of management to better the time limits given in the union-management agreement.

By studying the personnel files to learn an individual's preparation, aptitudes, hobbies, attitudes, and preferences, and by assisting in employee transfer procedures the counselor can help to insure that the best possible use is being made of each worker's abilities. Progressive management's search for potential supervisory personnel is a constant one. Who, if not the counselor, is better prepared to evaluate records and reports to determine where potential supervisory personnel is likely to be found? He also is in a position to encourage individuals who have demonstrated leadership qualities to obtain the necessary additional training for advancement.

If all situations in life could be fitted together and solved like the parts of a simple puzzle there would be few problems. When the individual finds that someone has placed a log across the path which leads to his goal, he must attempt to reach the goal by other routes or remove the obstacle. If his new attempts are not fruitful, he becomes increasingly alarmed and irritated as each new idea fails. Simply stated, here is the pattern of problem solving and its concomitants.

In the process of trying new routes to a given goal the individual may use a direct attack. The attempt might be compared to running at full speed in an attempt to jump over the log. In his direct attack, a pole vault might take the individual over the obstruction. The counselor can apply this simple illustration to problem solving by substituting mental activity for logs, pathways, and pole vaulting, and obtain a clear picture of what takes place in a worker's mind when the latter is blocked in his attempts to arrive at a satisfactory solution to a given problem.

Failing in his attempts to scale the object, the individual may plan a detour around it. He may try to go around both ends, pincer-style, or he may try one end and, failing, decide that it would be equally useless to try the other end.

Possibly *your* thinking is now ahead of your reading, and you are visualizing an individual attempting to cut his way through the barrier with axe and saw. You may picture the fellow who, at this point, just can't take it; he retreats into the woods to sit and rationalize. If confronted at this juncture, he would probably deny the fact that there is any obstacle blocking his pathway. If he admits having been blocked in his attempted travel towards his goal, he might say that he was not anxious to go farther at the time, anyway. You might learn how well his imagination works by listening while he paints a story of future hazards that make it much wiser to remain in his comfortable retreat.

After a period of time, the individual may decide that the goal is still to be desired, but that it is too difficult to achieve all at once. Consequently, with one eye on the goal and one eye on approaching inquirers, the individual attempts to justify his present position short of the goal. Here we see the "sour grapes" mechanism in action: the search for sympathy, the attempt to drown one's sorrow, and other evidences of frustration.

The counselor comes into the picture in an attempt to solve the problem. The counselor must know and understand the goal the counselee has in mind. Problem solving involves several well-defined steps. The first step involves getting all the facts. These facts may come from a review of the record of the individual and from conversations with him and his associates. Frequently an investigation of feelings and opinions may uncover some hidden fact not evident at first. Sometimes it is a misinterpretation of a posted notice or a printed policy. This probing technique should be continued until the counselor is certain that all the facts have been obtained. He is then in a position to assist the counselee in processing each fact objectively. Facts which evidently do not lead to the goal may be set aside, while those that fit together may be woven into a bridge of ideas leading towards the original goal. Several of these bridges, tentative courses of action, may be constructed. Here, the counselor can render a service to the individual by proposing more than one avenue which can be followed in solving the problem. The counselee must, of course, make the decision as to which avenue he will take. Thus, the counselor has performed one of his prime functions by helping the individual find avenues that lead towards the solution of a problem. A second service the counselor renders is that of explaining the technique of problem solving to counselees. The "weigh and decide" method can be demonstrated to the individual and he can be taught to distinguish an emerging pattern of action that will aid him.

If the counselor must help the individual to get started, the kind and amount of help needed should be decided upon. Properly timed action is also important to the solution of the problem. The counselor will want to follow-up to determine the results of his problem-solving technique. If the solution selected by the individual proved to be unsuitable, the suggested courses of action should be modified to bring the action and the objective into line once more. Through this procedure the counselor aids workers in problem solving.

Group problems are not unlike those of individuals. Employee participation in planning activities permits agreement and adjustment well in advance of the actual establishment of practices and procedures that affect their welfare. It is human nature to resist change, yet individuals accept it more readily if they have had a part in the planning. Every hour spent in promoting group planning will be returned, with interest, in the speed with which workers accept proposed changes.

The complexities of modern living have made indispensable to management, supervision, and workers the services of specialists in human relations problems. It is the challenging goal of the counselor to create and maintain harmonious relationships among the members of business and industrial organizations.

Questions

1. How was counseling used to advantage during World War II?
2. Name at least five factors to be kept in mind when counseling.

3. Name and discuss five guideposts which the counselor should remember.

4. Discuss the importance of understanding the plant and its product.

5. Why should a counselor know and understand the community?

6. How can he acquire this knowledge and understanding?

7. Why should a counselor understand federal, state, and local laws which affect the workers?

8. What is the value of understanding the job opportunities of the plant? Discuss the usefulness of this knowledge.

9. Discuss the use of tests and job analyses.

10. Would you like to be a counselor? Why? What preparation do you need?

Bibliography

Benge, Eugene J., *Maladjustment of Abilities and Interests,* Chapter IX, Society for the Psychological Study of Social Issues. New York: Gordon Co., Inc., 1940.

Scott, W. D., Clothier, R. C., Mathewson, S. B., and Spriegel, W., *Personnel Management.* New York: McGraw-Hill Book Co., 1941.

"Employee's Viewpoint Towards Personnel, Industrial Relations and Training," page 109. Purdue University, Engineering Extension Service Department Bulletin, Extension Series No. 45, Vol. XXIII, No. 6, November, 1939.

"Pay Envelope Is Not Employee's Greatest Concern," page 135. *Science News Letter,* Vol. 35, March 4, 1939.

Index

Index

Follow-up (*Cont.*):
  of placement of handicapped worker,
    65
  of rehabilitants, 50
  of special groups, 90
Foremen (*see* Supervisor)
Forms:
  physical capacities, 58
  physical demands, 59
Frost, Joseph H., 184
Fry, J. H., 125
Fuller, S. E., 41

G

Gardner, Burleigh B., 41, 98
General Electric Company, 146
Gibbs Underwear Company, 146
Giberson, Lydia G., 40, 125, 126, 131
G. I. Bill of Rights, 44, 76, 77, 228
Government Agencies, responsibility of,
    67
Greenberg, Virginia, 86
Graphic aids, 226
Greetings to the veteran, 74
Grievances:
  a program to cure, 170
  handling of, 109, 110, 115, 149, 211
  handling of (*footnote*), 215
Guidance:
  for veterans, educational, 79
  limitations of, 7
  of young people, 87, 88

H

Handicapped persons (*see* Worker)
Heyel, Carl, 141
Hibbs, Ray E., 125
Hildreth, Gertrude H., 98
Hiring:
  matching physical capacities with de-
    mands, 59
  procedure for, 10
  the physically handicapped, 18
Hitchcock, C. N., 162
Hoppock, R., 22, 141
Hoslett, S., 125
Houser, J. D., 22
Housing shortage a factor in counseling,
    93
Humm, D. G., 12

I

Incentives, 27, 28
Induction (*see also* Orientation):
  advantages of, 24
  definition of, 24
  of new counselor, 202-206
  of new employees, 111-113
  of women employees, 119
  responsibility of personnel department,
    24
  vs. orientation (*footnote*), 24
Industrial relations:
  improvement of, 12
  key to improved, 29
  needed changes, speed of making, 10
Influences, an important factor, 83
Injuries (*see also* Accidents):
  sideline, occupational, 29
Instructions to women, how to give, 95
International Resistance Company, 146
International Society for Crippled Chil-
    dren, 52
Interview:
  exit, 20, 121, 157
  follow-up, 113
Interviewing, technique of, 38, 82, 108,
    109, 114, 187, 190-192

J

Jager, Harry A., 219
Job:
  of counselor, 105
  matching physical capacities with de-
    mands of, 59
Job dissatisfaction (*see also* Worker dis-
    satisfaction):
  emotional factor (*footnote*), 9
  evidences of, 11
Job satisfaction, importance of, 9
Johnson, Lewis J., 197

K

Keller, Franklin J., 33
Kirkpatrick, Forrest H., 222
Knowles, Asa S., 162
Kosiak, Paul T., 165
Kraines, S. H., 93
Kratz, J. A., 66
Kushnick, William H., 100, 110